Deborah Bettega

SCREEN'S QUEEN

Screen's Queen
Copyright © 2023 by Deborah Bettega

All rights reserved. No part of this publication may be reproduced, distributed, or transmitted in any form or by any means, including photocopying, recording, or other electronic or mechanical methods, without the prior written permission of the author, except in the case of brief quotations embodied in critical reviews and certain other non-commercial uses permitted by copyright law.

Tellwell Talent
www.tellwell.ca

ISBN
978-0-2288-9112-3 (Hardcover)
978-0-2288-9111-6 (Paperback)
978-0-2288-9113-0 (eBook)

TO MY HUSBAND AND OUR SON

ABOUT THE AUTHOR

Deborah Bettega is a Russian-born, Italian and Australian small business owner. She spent her childhood between Italy and Russia before relocating to Australia in her early twenties.

She experienced mental health conditions and racism since her tender years, circumstances that led Deborah to be an advocate for inclusivity, equality and mental health awareness.

In Melbourne, she set up her business as a professional cleaner while continuing her mental health and well-being journey.

Deborah wants to tell her unique story and encourage anyone suffering from a mental health condition to seek professional help and promote attention to this topic.

Deborah currently lives in Melbourne with her husband, their son and their two cats.

This book is my personal recollection of events, and I have related them to the best of my knowledge. All the names, some details and some identities have been changed. This book contains material that might be a trigger due to the sexual assault issues described.

The following memoir is intended for entertainment use. It is a personal and unique story, so if any topic or event described raises any issue or discomfort, please seek a professional opinion.

TABLE OF CONTENTS

About the Author v
Chapter 1 Intro 1
Chapter 2 National Hotel 16
Chapter 3 Riverside 31
Chapter 4 Dacha 43
Chapter 5 Never Settle 54
Chapter 6 Be Kind 65
Chapter 7 Bad blood 83
Chapter 8 Angels 99
Chapter 9 Fear of addiction or addiction
             to fear? 117
Chapter 10 Offline 130
Chapter 11 Pandemic 146

CHAPTER 1

INTRO

Only when you lose everything will you be able to achieve anything.

I have always had certain beliefs about anxiety and depression, the first one being that I was among the very few to suffer from it. Nowadays, it is normal to speak about these conditions openly; however, when I was a child and a teenager, a strong stigma was present.

My mental health conditions have cost me a lot; I thought I was being broken, different, and damaged in a way.

Anxiety takes away your social life and your balance: you withdraw from all the social occasions and close into yourself because it is the easiest way. The idea of getting out sends your heart racing, and you break into sweats, secretly wishing the appointment or meeting gets cancelled.

Depression deeply undermines your body and mind. It creates a whirlwind of negativity and disturbing thoughts from which is hard to get out. It gives us a filter through which we see our reality as distorted, broken and hopeless. Physically your body aches from the inside. Your hands get tingly, and you are always so tired that getting out of bed daily seems impossible.

The highs are very high, but the lows are very low. Even in moments of stability, all you need is a trigger to go back to square one and relive all the traumas. A simple chat with someone or a completely normal circumstance in daily life is all it takes to trigger something in our scarred mind and get into a dark place once again.

I have learned that I am not alone in this battle only in recent years through my therapist and all the mental health advocates. Since that day, I have promised to be an advocate and speak out about the acceptance of mental health conditions. Only by using our voice can we raise awareness and overcome our fears.

Up until a couple of years ago, I had never felt accepted, understood, or had a sense of belonging. Children always pay the price of an unstable, broken parent who refuses to take responsibility for their actions.

My parents met in the mid-'80s in communist Russia. My Russian mother worked in the local post office in Volgograd, whilst my Italian father was in the same area to complete a big construction project.

My mother was an only child who had a strict traditional Russian childhood. She finished her studies when she was sixteen years old before moving to the capital city of Moscow for a life experience of a few years. She then returned to her native city; however, she always told me how uncomfortable she felt being close to and living with her parents. Since my childhood, I sensed that the family dynamic had not been of a caring, united and nurturing family.

On the other hand, my Italian father had a considerable age difference from my mother, had been previously married without having any children, and had a very tough post-war family upbringing. His parents passed away when he was a teenager. He had many siblings, and from an early age, he too decided to make his fortune elsewhere and started working for many construction companies across Europe first and then reaching Africa, the Middle East, and Russia.

My parents first saw each other at the post office; according to her, it was love at first sight. It is hard to know the truth now, but after many decades, I suspect that she first fell in love with the idea of escaping the Soviet Union. The idea of running away with a fascinating foreigner in order to create a life and a family in a different, Western country must have been appealing to many Russians.

The Soviet, or communist, Russia was a different reality from today. The USSR always had one great advantage: everyone felt the support of the state, however, there was total state control over all spheres of life. The workdays were the same for everyone; the school system was textbook for all the children across the nation, and a different thinking or mindset, was not possible.

There was a huge inaccessibility of information. Learning about world trends and events or gaining know-how on different topics was impossible.

Ownership of houses was abolished in the 1920s, during the early Soviet Union. Housing authorities determined who should live where. Large apartments and private houses were often remodelled into several smaller apartments, called *communalki*, or communal flats, which were the most popular type of public housing through the 80s.

Finally, there was a shortage of goods and culture. Long queues, particularly for bread, and limited availability ruled in every shop, from supermarkets to general stores, so this led to a big surge of black-market operations: usually, someone more successful, whose parents had the opportunity to make rare trips to other countries dealt with illegal but highly requested transactions.

On many occasions, nevertheless, the foreigners were controlled, followed, and blamed for espionage, which was a big deal in the Soviet Union. Often foreigners lived in controlled and designated areas, as my father did on his worksite, and even allocated marked cars.

On one occasion, when my parents were walking on the street, an official threatened them with a gun. Back then, in the 80s reality, a Russian woman should have nothing to do with a foreign man and find a local husband instead, and an Italian man should not pursue a romantic relationship with a local woman.

After dating for a few years, it was the time when my father's work project had come to an end, and this coincided with the discovery of the expectance of a child.

I was born in the city of Volgograd, in southwestern Russia, and when I was only forty days old, my parents and I moved permanently to my father's hometown—a small village in northern Italy.

My mother had never visited any part of Italy during those years of dating my father; hence this relocation was a recipe for disaster.

Italy is a very traditional and religious country. Back then, a foreigner or simply someone with a different lifestyle was not seen very well, and the integration was really hard, if not impossible. You either overcome it or break down.

Especially in little towns, the reality was very different from big cities; people were very traditional and narrow-minded and not open to any outsiders, let alone from a relatively distant country such as it was communist Russia.

I genuinely don't think my parents were ready to make this move as a family this suddenly.

Since the early days, my mother's arrival in this little town of around 10,000 residents had shocked many. She hadn't been accepted in the little reality of my hometown. Family members despised her behind her back. People talked and didn't act with kindness. On the contrary, they made her life difficult. Of course, this hatred towards the unknown was projected on me as well as a little kid.

Whilst my father had been regularly away for months due to work projects throughout my childhood years, my mother was a housewife and looked after me. Back in her hometown, she was very active workwise, having been recruited for several jobs, including tiler, bargain hunter for European tourists, and later, post office employee.

She really suffered because no one would offer her a job, and no one ever considered her applications as a translator for different local tourism initiatives, but everyone laughed about her accent and difficulty in learning the language at the beginning.

All those factors contributed to her fall into a long-lasting depression.

The topic of racism, furthermore, is never easy to talk or write about, even nowadays after the success of movements such as "Black Lives Matter."

As a little girl, having a mixed background didn't allow me to have a life like my classmates. I simply didn't fit in and was already starting a pattern that would follow me for most of my life. I always felt different, rejected. Deep down, I only wanted to feel normal.

Normal meant accepted, loved, cared about, and understood.

No one has ever been soft to me at home or outside, so the only way of life I knew was the hard one.

Throughout my school years, I was a target for bullies, an object of jokes, and struggled to build friendships. Having been born in Russia, even though I was, in fact, feeling and being raised mostly Italian, made me like a sort of a prank in the eyes of my classmates. As a child, I believe I had a mix of Russian and Italian aesthetic features, and I also spoke both languages.

My family and I kept moving or returning from Italy to Russia one way or another, so every time we had to start fresh, it was difficult as a little child.

At school, I also struggled to integrate. I was always the different one, the one everyone was curious about on the first days but put in the corner afterward. I was always classified as shy and introverted, but in reality, I only felt that I didn't fit in any box and was misunderstood. I was not Russian, but I was not Italian, either. I was not a geek but not among the popular students either. I was not from a wealthy family, but I was not poor.

Among the things I heard my new classmates saying about me were that I was a spy, that my parents were diplomats, or that we were undercover.

I still remember clearly a school recital in my primary school years featuring the theme of friendship and inclusivity. All the kids would dress and represent a country, embracing its colour, costume and culture for that occasion. In front of all the teachers and proud parents, every kid was exposing the principles of unity, acceptance and friendship without prejudice.

The meaning of the recital was to show and promote the importance of friendships based on equality, respect, and racial inclusivity. I also remember very well how I felt: hopeless, slapped in the face, and unhappy. Despite the meaningful values of acceptance and friendship without prejudice that had not been shown to me, I wondered how I could participate in the school recital.

The very same kids who had bullied me daily for reasons only linked by ignorance were the ones who had been picked to represent the more diverse, colourful, and geographically distant countries and were the ones preaching peace, love and fellowship. My little body of an eight or nine-year-old girl was already upside down, disgusted by the behaviour of my peers, behaviour that I thought I would only see in the movies.

I only wanted to scream to the world; however, I carried on with my battles in silence.

I had been allocated Russia as the country to represent, and for how much it felt like a cliché, this episode had been among the first times I was put in a box.

On that day probably, I realized that I did not like the world I was living in. So, in order to be happy, I would need to create a world that was good for me rather than live in one I would not fit in.

We are now so used to travel, relocation, work opportunities abroad, and the beginning of new ventures. However, in a country like Italy back then, this was something people rarely embarked on.

Having a mixed family was seen as something negative, something to hide and not to talk about. You would always present your parent from the nicer country first and secondly, the parent from the country or region classified as inferior.

On the contrary, in a country like Australia, having a multicultural background is an added value, something to be proud of and tell everyone about. It is a great pride to understand that the richer your family history is, the further your ancestors emigrated from, and the more you speak highly about your heritage.

I have lived all my life being an Italian in Russia, and a Russian in Italy, so basically considered a foreigner everywhere, despite being in my hometown in both cases. Now I perfectly understand that racism is present everywhere, as well as good people and bad people. However, in a multicultural country like Australia, I was just myself from day one and was welcome without any label.

According to my passports, I am Russian, Italian, and Australian, albeit I had lived most of my younger years in Italy before moving to Melbourne, Australia in my early twenties.

This is my story—a true and genuine autobiography of a young woman, proved by what life has thrown at her, battling mental health and racial biases while setting up her career as a professional housekeeper in Australia.

The rise of my cleaning company went parallel with the improvement of my mental health. The more I cleaned, the more I felt better about myself; the more I scrubbed, the more flaws I hid about myself, too.

When the pain was unbearable mentally, my physical pain seemed non-existent in contrast. But at last, the more I became conscious about my work, the less I started ignoring all the red flags of my mental health conditions, and I finally started my road to freedom.

Throughout the years, I have learned how to create positive energy from negative experiences and how to overcome personal traumas using negativity as fuel to create a better version of myself.

My therapy journey began in my early thirties in Melbourne, right before COVID-19 hit and the world was about to experience turmoil. I had been feeling particularly miserable and hopeless for a few months, so I knew something had to change. It had been a struggle waking up in the morning, functioning properly, working daily, and especially being around people. I felt like everyone was my enemy and that there was a conspiracy against me. I had to defend myself from everything and everyone. Even just talking with someone could easily lead me to a discussion, and clearly, I could not go on like that.

I had not reached a "breaking point," such as a nervous breakdown, which often occurs when our mind tells us that it cannot endure anymore. It was as if, without knowing exactly what to do, I had an internal force that led me in the right direction. A key factor was my general practitioner: a young, efficient, and skilled doctor with a special interest in mental health. He was not my doctor for long; in fact, my GP was another doctor working at the same clinic, who relocated, so his patients had been automatically allocated to the other practitioners in that clinic.

So, I scheduled an appointment with my new doctor, and after hearing about my struggle, straight away, he strongly suggested that I start psychology therapy. My mood, my patience and my mental health were so poor that I accepted his advice and referral.

My GP did not know any therapist available without a considerable waiting list, so I started my own research. I found relatively quickly the professional who became my psychologist for the long run and to whom I am beyond grateful and thankful.

My very first appointment felt like a weight I had carried for nearly thirty years, lifting off my shoulders. The result of the first session was that I was suffering from depression and severe anxiety, which also led me to have trust issues and a mild obsessive-compulsive disorder. The start of everything has been attributed to the emotional abuse I was exposed to in my family.

By no means is my story a professional teaching guide or suggesting mental health advice. My goal is to share my story, speak up about a topic that has been considered shameful for way too long, and help whoever is struggling to realize their potential. It's okay not to feel okay. If you are having a hard time, the best thing to do is seek professional help and start your own journey to well-being.

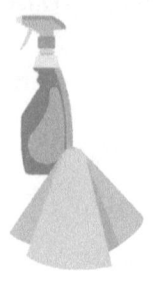

CHAPTER 2

NATIONAL HOTEL

I have always liked cleaning. I was brought up to be independent since I was young, so as early as eight or nine years old, I did everything on my own. Juggling between two countries, I had to adapt quickly to new schedules, different routines, and diverse lifestyles and societies.

When I was in Russia, I had to behave like a grown-up teenager because there, society leads you to independence soon. Whilst in Italy, children usually mature slower, lingering in the warmth of the family for much longer. I didn't have the privilege of the latter.

Since my primary school years in Italy, I prepared by myself, walked to school by myself, and many times cooked meals for myself; hence cleaning and organizing have always been part of my everyday schedule. My father was often away for work projects abroad, and my mother had been fighting her own demons on and off. Nevertheless, I did not have grandparents in Italy or any relatives to count on. I had no one to rely on, so I had to be my own parent.

These circumstances led me to incarnate the perfect representation of a lone wolf—a person who enjoys being alone rather than in company just for the sake of it. That is also the reason I learned very early how to rely only on myself.

Despite everything, I consider myself a strong person. When you don't have any choice, the only option is to be tough.

The problem, however, is that we cannot be the strongest person every time; we have moments of weakness, too. Battling mental health since early childhood means constantly having two voices inside your head; like in the movies, the angel tells you to be good and forgiving and to carry on being a good person. However, the little devil tells you to give up, that you are a failure, worthless, and will not achieve anything good in life.

A great lesson I received from my grandparents is to have discipline. The ability to carefully control how we work, live, or behave gives us a sense of commitment to our actions and makes us achieve a goal quickly.

Discipline creates habits; habits make routines and daily routines become who you are. The value of discipline is the way to do what needs to be done. Not only does practice allow one to establish a positive action, but it also helps us train our minds and body and enables us to focus on our goals and regulate our emotions.

No matter how hard things would get in life, I would still wake up in the morning, make my bed and do one hundred abs exercises in order to be ready for the day.

Another significant principle I have learned since an early age is the importance of independent thinking. Not having any remarkable role model around me made me take the habit of making my own decisions independently, without the influence of family, friends, colleagues, or personal upbringing.

Nowadays, it is very hard to have a personal opinion. We are influenced literally every hour of our lives, mostly by social media, but also by the people close to us, and I believe that it is fundamental to do our own research, weigh the pros and cons, and make rational decisions based only on our own opinion and experience.

Being raised independently from a very early age, I consider myself an advocate for independent thinking. This means having a strong mindset, led by facts and past experiences and without the predominant influence of family, friends, institutions, or random theories.

The figure of a role model is a person whose behaviour, mindset, and actions are imitated by others. Having a figure to admire is important from early childhood. An important role model I had in the last decade is the Formula 1 champion, Lewis Hamilton. First, he is a kind, humble, and driven human being. He is also an extraordinary, energetic and ambitious athlete, among the greatest of all time in his field.

Lewis has a mixed-race background, so I can relate to him and understand perfectly the struggles that he also faced in his childhood and early professional karting days. He comes from a humble family, so he knows that nothing comes on a silver plate; hence he promotes the values of hard work, practice, and patience. Furthermore, Lewis has a soft spot for disadvantaged people, children and teenagers with backgrounds of colour, and the communities in need. Hence, he is always on the line by making charity donations, setting up programs to help the most vulnerable communities, and doing everything in his power to fight racism.

On my hardest days, I can confidently state that Lewis and his vision helped me overcome my difficulties. Thinking about his values, positivity and achievements made me focus on the good things and gave me the thrive to do better and be better for the people I love.

* * *

I started working in Italy in my late teens, at first during the summertime break from school, and in nearly all my past jobs, I performed cleaning tasks.

I first moved to Australia in my early twenties. For many reasons, I have never pictured myself living in Italy forever, so the opportunity to explore a different country came up for my husband and me. The beginning had been far from easy. First, I underestimated how distant Australia is and how long it takes to get there by plane. We landed in the hottest days of summer, right when the European winter was in full bloom. It took me about ten days only to recover from the jet lag. Being a person following a routine on pretty much a daily basis, the beginning had been very hard for me. First, a totally different season did not help, considering that I have a low tolerance for the heat. Although Italy is a country with very warm summers, I had been living in northern Italy, in a mountain resort, so a relatively cold area.

Despite being used to living between two countries, having unexpected travels, and starting over in a different reality, I had difficulty settling in Melbourne. Everything seemed so distant and diverse from the places I knew. I remember that after only a few weeks, I really wanted to return to Italy, once again feeling that I didn't fit in, and I really felt out of place, with the only difference being that the trip to Europe would have been way longer.

The initial contrast between the two countries was also strong—Italians are loud and vibrant, using amicable gestures and speaking a lot, while in Australia, people normally are extremely friendly but do not have the need to speak at the same volume. Nevertheless, like most European countries, Italy holds so much culture, history, museums, and general historical knowledge that Australia lacks as a relatively young country without many historical events.

When you try so hard for so long, starting from zero one more time feels like an impossible task, and all the demons fought in the past begin to reappear.

I was in a particularly bad place mentally. In fact, within a few months, I had gained weight due to stress and an unhealthy diet. I managed to find a few different hospitality jobs; apparently, the only job I could be hired for had been washing dishes in cafes.

I did not have a university degree, and as of today, I sort of regret this.

During my last years of high school, I was clearly led to believe that I would not have the support or the resources from my family to enrol at university.

After finishing high school, I moved back to northern Italy to live on my own, though the closest university was around 100 kilometres away from my town, naturally without the possibility of studying remotely that we have today.

Despite that, I would soon experience an unexpected turn of events that would make it simply impossible to start a university journey, even with the strongest will.

But back to my first experience Down Under—I had managed not to surrender, as usual, finding a strength within that told me not to give up just yet. My husband and I had decided to relocate to Perth, the capital city of Western Australia.

My cultural background is from two very neat countries; we really look after our homes and pay attention to details.

I knew the worth of my trade and experience. I had been thinking of setting up my own housekeeping company for a while, specializing in cleaning luxury homes.

On one of our first nights of that new life experience in Perth, I wanted to break the news to my husband to see his thoughts on this. A business idea always comes with fears, doubts, and many questions. Being employed in a company has many perks, including regular shifts, secure pay, and a payslip. On the other hand, setting up a company would allow me to be my own boss, choose my clientele, and set my own terms and conditions, but the financial stability would arrive with time, certainly not at the beginning. Calibrating the pros and cons of both scenarios is normal for everyone, as is having many questions and uncertainties.

My husband, however, had been blown away by my idea and fully supported me since day one.

Not only was I good at cleaning, but the business idea had lots of potential; in Australia, houses are generally spacious, so families are very likely to look for and hire a cleaner to help their households. Furthermore, when people work full time, it becomes very hard to clean up by themselves, so hiring a helper with the house chores is very normal.

At the time, we had been living temporarily at a friend's house while looking for our own place. This big and charming home was located in the northern suburbs of Perth, had four bedrooms, a big living room, and featured a huge backyard with a pool. The brother of our lovely friend and host had been running his own gardening business, so he had given me so many precious tips, insights, and advice, and I owe him a lot.

The very next day, I opened my Australian business number, a unique number, in order to be registered as a sole trader and work lawfully for myself.

At this point, my first task was to promote my business and create my client portfolio. I chose a nice design for my business cards, as I believe that a great presentation is everything; there is no second chance to make a good first impression. One of the basic rules is to write my name clearly (obvious to me but not obvious at all as half of the requests I have received did not contain the requestor's name) and the type of services I offered.

Even nowadays, some people are positively shocked when I hand them my business card, which proves my point.

A good way of doing marketing for a new business is surely online. There are many platforms to advertise a trade or the old-fashioned way of advertising in local papers and supermarket boards.

For how I decided to work from the beginning, though, one of the best methods was word of mouth. When you find a new client who is happy with how you work, they are very likely to recommend you to a friend, relative or colleague.

I still remember my first client as a sole trader cleaner: a nice couple in their late twenties-early thirties who had been traveling through the summer holidays, so their home had been neglected and needed some attention. Their home was a two-bedroom loft townhouse, and based on their quick description, we agreed on three hours of work.

On the day no one was home, the clients left me the keys under the mat outside, so I let myself in. I had a look around, and lastly, reaching the bathroom, I broke down in tears.

I instantly called my husband, who tried to calm me down and made my panic attack disappear. Gasping for air, I tried to explain the state of that house and that three hours wouldn't have been enough for half of the property.

After a few minutes, I calmed down, and I did what I had been used to in life: compose myself, remind myself of how strong my willpower is, and get started on the job.

I called the clients, explaining that it would be very hard to get everything done properly in the allocated time, asked them what to prioritize, and reassured them that I would do my best.

Not only had their townhouse been messy and neglected, but it also had lots of indoor plants that brought insects and left dry leaves around the whole living area. The place had an unpleasant smell of a space being closed for too long and old rotten food, and the dust in the lofted bedrooms was so much that it created a grey coat on every surface. The kitchen was an explosion of dry stains over the walls, cooking stove, and cabinets.

Lastly, the bathroom was in an unforgivable state and had a nauseating smell of sewerage. A mixture of soap, hair, and dust covered the sink top. I couldn't see myself clearly in their mirror. In the showers, there were algae. The majority of the products that I had brought weren't powerful enough, so I had to scrub all the surfaces three or four times.

I am still trying to wrap my head around thinking of that experience and how I managed to get that result in only three hours. Normally rental properties have routine inspections from real estate agents, which are helpful to assure that the properties are looked after properly and are in overall good condition. After a few years, however, these routine inspections might even drop to one or two in-person inspections per year, depending on the type of agency. It is still a mystery to me how this property had reached such a bad state; however, my experience allows me to state that there is no set time in order to mess a home to a certain level.

Later that evening, the clients were extremely happy, thanked me, and left me a tip. I had worked at their home a few more times on a fortnightly basis before they moved to a different location.

During that period, I had many requests for one-off cleans. Those types of cleans were predominantly end-of-lease cleanings, meaning they were requested by the real estate agents on lease contracts when the tenants had to vacate a property. One-off cleans could also mean spring cleans: a more detailed, major cleaning service done, as suggested, in the springtime to freshen up the house before the summer season.

Those opportunities usually meant better money, but I had started to prioritize and accept only regular jobs.

On the one hand, end-of-lease cleaning was always a surprise, people always said that they were pretty tidy, and then once in the property, it happened that it was so messy, or the place was so spacious that I had to come back the day after to finish the work. On the other hand, I have always liked a routine, so regular jobs fit me perfectly, even sacrificing slightly on my wage.

I soon realized that I needed structure in my business, and by the time I had taken this decision, I already had a few regular clients on my schedule, so it was difficult to have a gamble every week and accept one-off jobs.

Soon enough, though, I realized that in order to accept and commit to a job, I needed to go further and started to introduce a quick "meet and greet" with a potential new client.

This simply consisted of a quick chat at the client's house, so we had the opportunity to get to know each other. The clients were able to show me their property while I took notes of their different requests, needs, and different surfaces and features of their homes.

At the end of this informal chat, we would have an idea if I would be a perfect addition to their household and hence able to commit on a long-term basis.

Most of the time, this meeting was a success, and to this day, I am still adapting this system as my golden rule.

CHAPTER 3

RIVERSIDE

Since I was a little kid, I have always believed in gender equality end equal opportunities for everyone, regardless of gender firstly, but also of religion, background, and social status.

Nowadays, we have large access to any kind of free international channels, broadcast, and media coverage, but in the 1990s, the situation was different, and the international channels required more effort to have access to. So, I believe that these strong values I hold today began during my childhood, thanks to my family owning an international pay-per-TV antenna, which we installed so my mother could watch the Russian TV channels while living in Italy during the 90s.

During the afternoons, I remember watching many international (mostly

American) programs and series in which the society looked so different, so far away from the reality of my little hometown that I knew so well. In these programs, the family dynamics were diverse, many women worked, even held important positions, and were considered an important asset to society, so I took great inspiration from these television shows.

Today, sadly, Italy is still a very male-dominated society. However, I simply couldn't understand why, back then, like nowadays, women were confined to the role of stay-at-home mums or housewives in the society I was living in. I remember saying to my parents that one day I would be a successful working woman, earning my own money, and unfortunately, I wasn't the only girl who had received the answer, "well then, marry a rich man!"

Once again, having different ideas and an open mindset wasn't something people understood. If they can't put you in a box, they start judging you, laughing at you, and isolating you.

When I was in my teenage years, my family and I relocated to a little town in central/

northern Italy. Even later, as a teenager in my high school years, my beliefs as a young feminist grew up as fast as did my awkwardness in social contexts.

My schoolmates couldn't understand my stance in a society predominantly led by men. As a result, I didn't have many relationships during high school. Simply talking to someone from the opposite gender gave me unease. I remember constantly thinking, "this is so wrong" or "this shouldn't be acceptable."

If I wasn't getting the amount of respect that I wished, then I wasn't interested— whether it was a friendship or more than that.

People said I was difficult, but I kept speaking up and standing for my values. They said I was being complicated; I kept pretending to respect. They told me I was too much; I kept on taking my space.

I didn't need to prove anything to anyone or pretend to be someone I wasn't just to be liked or pleased by others.

When you are used to relying only on yourself, people might be intimidated by your confidence. Sadly, sometimes people pretend you're a bad person, so they don't feel guilty about how they treat you.

Traumas teach you to be tough and to pursue your own integrity, so I didn't really care about other people's opinions.

In Italy, every day, I am reminded of the struggle of just being a woman in modern society. For starters, the wage for the same work position is different. A woman must work double for a way lesser payslip. Generally speaking, family expectations are not equal. If you are a woman, the family expects you to be a caring mum sooner or later and give up slowly on your career as if to say a man's profession cannot be sacrificed, but a woman's can be.

Furthermore, there is a general annoying custom in the male's mindset to give very often unwanted and insistent attention to women. Catcalling is rude, unflattering, and extremely offensive. I believe that every single woman in Italy has ever experienced that; it is so wrong and should not be acceptable.

We should, lastly, remember that feminism doesn't mean being anti-men. Feminism means equal treatment, opportunities, respect for all genders, and standing up for everyone's basic rights.

* * *

Among my role models, I also include the digital consultant and ambassador, Xenia Tchoumi. A pioneer in gender equality battles and feminism in recent years, she is a published author. Xenia is a digital entrepreneur and a public speaker with an economics degree. In fact, she turned down a very appealing offer to work for a leading investment bank in order to achieve her goal of setting up her own business as a lifestyle and fashion digital consultant.

I can resonate with her. First, for proudly being a feminist. She also has a Russian and Italian background and speaks six languages. I admire her strong mindset and her principles: I am, as well, used to following my gut and being true and consistent to myself.

In moments of self-doubt or when I am overwhelmed by the amount of discrepancy women have to endure nowadays in every field, I take great comfort in supporting her battles, following her fiercely independent lifestyle and precious life-changing suggestions for modern women. Xenia's advice and life tricks are highlighted in her book *Empower Yourself: How to Make Lemonade When Life Gives You Lemons,* and I cannot relate more to every word written in her guide to female empowerment.

Contrary to the Italian reality I knew, it was a breath of fresh air when I first arrived in Australia. I could instantly sense an overall spirit of respect, gender equality, and a society based on merit.

While living Down Under, I do not recall ever experiencing any kind of discrimination as a woman, not on a personal level or workwise.

* * *

I still remember so clearly the day I received Peter's call. It was a pleasant and sunny summer's day, and I had just finished my shift at my hospitality part-time job. It was the beginning of my cleaning company, and I had decided to continue my other employment in a casual but contemporary café. The staff was lovely, and I had such a great time working there!

So, due to my lack of free time, I wasn't used to answering too many work calls. However, I was in a great mood after a particularly efficient day that day, so I decided to take that call.

Peter was an employee of a transport company and sounded very easy-going and polite. Along with his partner Erin, he was looking for a fortnightly cleaning lady for their apartment in the inner city of Perth.

He also insisted on telling me that it was very difficult to find a reliable housekeeper or even a professional who answered promptly to their request. I didn't really pay that much attention to this detail, for giving an answer as quickly as possible was simply polite and a staple of common sense.

We booked the usual meeting for one of the next days. Erin and Peter's apartment was a two-bedroom, two-bathroom spacious, bright and modern apartment located in one of the tall buildings facing the Swan River.

They were a normal-looking couple without children in their fifties, and during the meeting, they confidently handed me the keys to their apartment.

I worked three or four times when, one morning, I noticed a different vibe, that something was off. Erin had never been present at home during my services, and Peter usually got out of the apartment once I arrived and started my chores.

That morning, I also noticed Peter was still in his robe instead of normal clothes, but I figured that it could happen since it must have been earlier in the morning than usual on that day.

I was still assembling the vacuum and sorting out my products when, after a few minutes, Peter walked into the living room in front of me, completely naked and clearly aroused.

What followed was a blur. The time in my mind had stopped; it could have been one second or one hour that passed. I don't normally lose my composure, but I was totally in shock and unable to move. I remember being scared that my moment had arrived.

I remember thinking that the best scenario was that I would be raped. The worst scenario was that I would die on that day. I remember that horrible and mortifying feeling that only a woman can ever experience: vulnerability, weakness, and powerlessness.

The first thing I remember doing was calling my husband. Luckily, my phone was in my pocket, and I decided to take the chance of using it and ask him to come and pick me up as soon as possible. I thought I sounded pretty in shock, but I also tried successfully to sound casual and calm; the worst thing to do, I thought, was to show fear to your predator. My husband did not suspect that something was off and was running an errand in the opposite part of the city. Running away wasn't an option either, as the lift in the building was quite slow, and I thought that this would make things even worse. On top of that, I also had to carry my products and equipment, bought with my hard-earned savings.

My husband collected me later, in a couple of hours, as scheduled.

I was still shocked and miserable after the call to my husband, but probably something about my attitude suggested also not to mess with me. Peter left his apartment in a few minutes without making any move or saying a word to me, and I never saw him again.

Somehow, I found the courage to finish the cleaning session, even though I had trouble standing up, looking around me, and determining if something had already been tidied up or not. I am still trying to figure out how I maintained a calm and collected mind and finished the job.

In most cases, after sexual harassment, a woman asks herself what she did wrong. Was it a smile, a word said in a cheeky way, or was it simply that friendly tone during the first call?

This certainly didn't apply to me. I wasn't feeling a single drop of guilt. I knew I had done absolutely nothing wrong. I was and still am a professional, offering my trade in an honest way, while Peter was a sick, perverted individual, and that is completely on him.

I have reasons to believe that Erin knew about these deviant dynamics, and perhaps even enjoyed being part of it. I don't even think

I was the first or the only cleaning lady who experienced that in the couple's household.

While I was still processing and unable to think clearly, my husband, who had been very supportive and extremely concerned about my well-being, suggested that this was a clear case of sexual harassment in the workplace and should be addressed.

So, we went to the local police station and explained the situation to an officer. He listened carefully to what had happened and looked him up in the system. He was not able to disclose if he had a record, but I expressed my wish to press charges against Peter and asked about the proceedings.

I prepared all the paperwork to press charges for sexual harassment, and everything was ready to start the legal process. However, shortly before that, my husband and I decided to relocate back to Melbourne due to a job opportunity.

The process could have been nasty, long and expensive. At first, I was disappointed; all I wanted was justice and to stand up for my principles.

Perth is a stunning city with a warm climate, wild nature, relaxed lifestyle, and room for lots of opportunities. However, the latest dramatic event did not encourage us to continue our journey in Western Australia.

This episode happened before the infamous "Me Too" movement. Speaking up and telling the truth was different back then. The process could have been distressing in the long run.

Sometimes having closure and moving on is more important than fight. The hard decision taken, indeed, was to give up on the charges and relocate to Melbourne in order to progress rather than being stuck in that dark moment of sexual harassment for years.

When someone has struggled with mental well-being for most of their life, a dramatic experience triggers lots of negativity. I wondered what next, I would experience: wasn't it enough? When would I have peace?

I still remember that familiar taste in my mouth, the bittersweet taste of failure, disappointment, and insecurity.

It was clear that I needed one more closure, so starting fresh once again was the perfect opportunity.

CHAPTER 4

DACHA

Many people have asked me how to start and run a cleaning or a similar business in trades. This was the desire of many but the reality of a few.

The truth is that there is no shortcut to success. I started with a simple idea, gaining lots of information and only with my husband's support. Many people are unwilling to do the hard job and expect to find a ready-to-eat meal, but it doesn't work like that. A business idea requires lots of dedication, time, sacrifices, and ultimately, only you can lead in the right way.

When I was a little kid, during my Russian summer holidays in the 1990s, I had been staying for several weekends at the family Dacha. A Dacha is like a farmhouse, with a generous lot of greenery outside the big cities where families come to relax, recharge their batteries, and spend quality time with family and friends.

My grandparents were traditional Russian orthodox: they grew up in a society led by communism in the Soviet Union. They knew loyalty, diligence, camaraderie, and conventionalism as native values, yet they did not know a world populated by hate and malicious people.

I only have wonderful memories of my time spent at the Dacha, mostly with my grandparents: even preparing all the food and supplies was an enjoyable task. I could see the excitement in my grandparents' eyes after having done the grocery shopping for fresh bread at the Eastern European delicatessen and some chocolate lollies for all the kids of the neighbourhood Dachas. The trip usually took around one hour or so, and I remember looking outside the window in the back seat of the car. I admired the shift from the crowded and grey streets of the city to the huge fields and the greenery when the rural precincts were approaching.

The arrival was as magical as the stay. For the adults, the entrance to the Dacha's little and simply made country houses, usually located on one corner of the land, was a strict routine made of picking up and organizing all the shopping bags and baskets of supplies and sorting out the electrical generator due to the frequent thefts of copper present in many electrical wires. However, in the eyes of little kids, the start of the stay was as serene as walking on a cloud. To me, it felt like a joyful moment and the beginning of a weekend of bonding with mother nature. One of the first things I remember doing was having a quick walk through the thin concrete pathways that led from one little field to another, looking at the progress of all the plump and fresh vegetables, admiring all the colourful fruits on the trees and inhaling all the scents, from coriander to fennel, passing through basil and mint.

In the Dacha, pretty much everything was handmade by the owners, beginning with the little homes. The furniture was usually old items from the main city apartments; the cabinets were always handmade from pieces of wood. Whoever was lucky enough to have a gas stove for all the cooking brought little jars of gas, and the water was from an external little tank, usually brought from the drinking water tank in the nearest rural town. The bathroom was very rudimentary— basically, a toilet handmade around a hole in the ground, with wooden and steel panels for privacy. We also had a very comfortable shower and a sink. There was a tank in the little roof of the shower, so during summer, the water would be very warm, enough for a well-deserved shower.

This lifestyle would probably be very hard to understand nowadays in Western society; however, I consider myself lucky as it taught me many lessons such as adapting to every environment, being handy and flexible, solving many problems, and most importantly, understanding the value and luck of living in a home with many comforts and luxuries.

Among the many fun activities enjoyed by the locals at the Dachas, the most popular ones were having long chats with comrades over a nice drink, playing games, and preparing the *shashlik*, which is basically a barbecue prepared with mixed meat marinated with a mixture of fresh and zesty herbs.

One of the sweetest memories of my childhood is playing cards with my grandma, who was the undisputed boss of a Russian card game called "the idiot"; in fact, she had hardly let me win a game!

Highly coveted poker nights with the Dacha's neighbours were held frequently—an adults-only event during which focus, and silence dominated the living area. We children were upstairs, playing or telling each other stories. The hosting of the poker night was a serious affair, too, it followed a strict schedule among the neighbourhood participants, and it involved special preparations: from the best vodka, brought from the city to the finger food refreshments ordered in the local deli with a week's advance, in order to impress and welcome all the guests.

Despite being a place designated for fun times, many people, especially pensioners, treated these duties in the Dacha as a full-time job. On top of the maintenance of the houses, there were trees and plants, vegetables and fruits to be looked after. As a result, elderly people with bigger properties saw the harvesting of fresh seasonal produce as an opportunity for income.

Buyers from the big cities arrived every week on the main squares of these little rural towns. They were interested in purchasing boxes, buckets, and cassettes of fresh tomatoes, apricots, strawberries, and every kind of genuinely grown product.

I helped my dedicated grandparents with some light harvesting duties, so it was fair that I would get a little of the sum earned by selling those fruits and vegetables. This way, I would have some change in order to buy ice cream with my summer friends or save it to make a gift for my grandparents. This had also been the beginning of my economic ventures and entrepreneurial spirit.

Another way of making some pocket money while having fun and helping the neighbourhood was to collect empty bottles from the streets. Local glass warehouses were usually located in selected basements, and they accepted empty bottles of soft drinks, beer and wine. In exchange, they offered a few *kopeiki*, the Ruble's cents.

This activity was very popular among problematic and disadvantaged individuals, as well as among kids and teenagers, recruited and supervised on specific days by building managers or local associations. In both cases, it was a good way to help and keep the community tidy and a lesson in responsibility, hard work, and common sense.

On the other hand, what I consider to be my hometown, is a lovely and charming little valley in the heart of the Dolomite Mountains, located in northern Italy, not to be confused with my birthplace in the Russian city of Volgograd.

Growing up, during my primary school years, I mostly lived in Italy, and usually, during the summertime, I stayed with my mother and grandparents in Russia at their place.

I didn't have many deep friendships in my primary school years, so I have found a connection with nature rather than with people. I remember going on long walks with my mother, exploring the local gardens, and being amazed by the breathtaking scenery of the mountains. I did not understand why there could possibly be so much hate in such a beautiful world.

It is possible to practice numerous sports and outdoor hobbies in my hometown. Cycling is a very popular activity in my hometown during summertime and colder months. I remember, when I was a kid, there was a very popular mountain bike competition, divided into the adult and children's versions. It was very coveted among the residents and even attracted many tourists.

In wintertime, though, there are many more activities to do and sports to practice in a mountain resort. Aside from the most popular— skiing, cross skiing and snowboarding— there are hiking and ice skating. I was particularly attracted to the latter two in my tender years, so I enjoyed hiking on snow-white trails or ice skating at the local outdoor rink.

I can relate to the words of the wise Nelson Mandela, who once said: "After climbing a great hill, one only finds that there are many more hills to climb."

* * *

One of the key lessons for someone who wants to start a business and offer their trade in Australia in recent years is to understand what locals want. Having the mindset and work schedule as it had been in our home country wouldn't bring consistency.

Through the years, I have seen many newly arrived fellow Italians behaving and having such lifestyles as they would have in their native country without any lasting success.

Another popular pattern in certain cultures, including Greek and Italian, was to hang out only among compatriots. This includes living in the same house, spending their free time together, or working together.

If I had a dollar for every time someone had said to me, "I will discover new cultures and avoid people from my own country," despite ending up doing the exact opposite, I would be rich by now.

Respecting my roots is obviously very important, but to me personally, there was no point in having an active part in everything Italian. If I wanted to live fully Italian, I would have lived in Italy.

Luckily, my mixed origins allowed me to have an open mind since the beginning of my Australian days, so I was eager to discover the multicultural beauty of Melbourne and what was on the other side of my fears and worries.

From my personal and professional point of view, in most of my jobs, Australian clients want a home clean and fresh, where everything is neat and in order, but not necessarily all the details of a proper deep cleaning. The priority is often to return to a tidy and organized home with a freshly made bed, the kid's room clear of toys, and the laundry and dishwasher taken care of, like in a professionally staged home.

I remember one time I worked in this beautiful sky-rise apartment, and the first time, to impress the new customer, I cleaned every detail and corner from top to bottom. Only to find out that the client had noticed only that the pillows on the couch weren't put on in a pretty way.

Then I learned that a normal cleaning could not include every little detail, such as wiping the skirting boards, wiping remote corners, removing marks on the walls (unless very evident), or wiping inside the cupboards and cabinets. These tasks had to be included in a special deep clean upon agreement with the client.

With great pleasure, I remember that through the years, my role wasn't confined to being only a cleaning lady: occasionally, I was a personal assistant, nanny, pet carer, and personal stylist (the perks of having an Italian housekeeper with a sense of style!)

Many times, I was also a sort of property manager, letting various technicians inside my clients' houses and showing them what needed to be fixed. Once, I even recruited a gardener for a client who urgently needed a tidy-up in the small backyard and entrance, and good gardeners are difficult to find.

CHAPTER 5

NEVER SETTLE

After relocation from Perth to Melbourne, I struggled to find long-term work opportunities. Back then, I had been living in a very central area of the city, close to the central business district. Surely it was a very busy and populated area, full of tall apartment complexes, but I was finding it difficult to gain regular jobs. The area offered lots of properties on Airbnb or similar short-term accommodation services, but even so, I was convinced to follow my principles and carry on with my weekly and fortnightly only cleaning services.

Needless to say, people responded to my advertisements from the most faraway suburbs from my location, asking about all kinds of services but the ones I offered, such as end-of-lease cleaning. Furthermore, it is still a mystery to me why many people think that light gardening or looking after plants is a cleaner's task.

In many fields in life, I have noticed that people understand only what they want. I am only responsible for what I say or write, not what people might understand.

By then, I already had a certain degree of experience and understanding of the Australian market regarding my field. I had meetings without getting the job I hoped for or applied for work opportunities without hearing back from the other end. At that point, though, I realized something important: I was overqualified for a particular position rather than underqualified.

Having had a background of trust issues, a potential rejection is never an easy pill to digest. However, thanks to my therapy journey, I realized that in most cases, the infamous worst-case scenario is only created in our mind, and there are many different reasons why it's possible not to hear back from someone.

Furthermore, the fact that I had started to react so well compared to my old self made me really proud and content.

This episode reminded me of an English course I was going to undertake in my early twenties. I had the luck of being resident in a very rich and resourceful region of northern Italy, famous for having many local funds and grants, such as the possibility to take an English short course, complete with a weekend trip to Dublin, upon completion. I was instantly interested and signed up for this opportunity, even though I had already studied, knew, and spoke some English.

However, the upcoming relocation to Australia made me hungrier for knowledge of the local language, and I was already picturing myself improving thanks to that course. Furthermore, a short trip to Dublin, a capital city I had been drawn to and interested in, was appealing. In that moment, I was looking forward to visiting St Patrick's Cathedral, discovering the Irish culture and drinking a pint of Guinness beer in the pub owned by one of my favourite rock bands, the local U2.

There was a quick assessment prior to the start of the English course, but for me, it had been as simple as having a glass of water. I was the first to finish the task and was confident that nearly all my answers were correct.

There was no notice of the entry-level requirements, and with great disbelief and disappointment, I discovered that my scores were too good. I was not suitable to participate in the course because my English level was too proficient. In fact, I completed the assignment fully and correctly; hence I did not need to perfect my knowledge of English according to whoever managed this program.

I did not take it well. I started screaming and crying as soon as I got home. Once again, one trigger is all it takes to go back to a dark place that enables a cycle of negativity and a sense of failure. How was it possible that I had been among the best in completing the assignment and I did not get a spot in the class? It took me many years to understand that I had been overqualified for that English course and how I am today overqualified for certain jobs.

Another double-edged sword in my field is represented by clients' referral to a friend, colleague or relative by word of mouth. This could be a great opportunity for a perfect job in the perfect location, or it could be the complete opposite. In this case, it is crucial to be polite but honest in order to not overcommit to a job that could potentially put off my schedule.

What I still love the most about a regular cleaning schedule is the relationship built with my clients, the sense of reciprocal trust, and of course, seeing the results of my detailed work, week after week.

Soon enough, the right opportunities arrived, and I was hired by Jessica, a friendly mother of two and director of a company in the tourism industry.

By that time, I still hadn't got my own car, so I had to filter all the requests based on location and public transport. The cleaning equipment at that point was always provided by the clients, according to their needs, so I only had to carry with me a basket with my go-to products, gloves, cloths, and essentials.

After a while, when receiving a job request, I had perfected the ability to feel if that job would be in the well-connected part of that particular suburb, and somehow, I was rarely wrong. For Jessica and her family, I would have to clean her house and office, both in the inner suburbs of Melbourne and conveniently on my tram route.

During the initial meeting, I saw the office I would clean every week, and we had the usual quick acquaintance.

The office was in a very charming Victorian-style house, and the cleaning would be scheduled during business hours, which was very unusual. Vacuuming and dusting around while the employees were in full business swing wasn't ideal, but this schedule also meant more convenient hours for me.

Jessica's house was also located nearby, and it was a big, provincial-style house with five bedrooms, four bathrooms, and with very classy furniture and finishing. The family also had a live-in au-pair who had been helping them look after the kids. The figure of the au-pair generally helps and assists the kids in the everyday life; she may drop and pick up the kids from school, help them with their homework, play with them, prepare snacks or light meals, and organize their rooms, beds, and wardrobes. Depending on the contract, they should also be able to organize their school uniforms, tidy their rooms and put away all their toys.

When I first started at Jessica's, as usual, I needed a few shifts to get to know the house and learn where all the products and equipment were, being it a very large house.

Every time I also got to know the adorable au-pair, a very caring and organized girl who genuinely looked after the kids.

After a few weeks, however, her contract ended, and their new au-pair moved in. Contrary to the incumbent, the new girl was messy, distant, and had a general feeling of untidiness. At times, she seemed distracted with the kids and certainly wasn't cooperating with her allocated chores.

I have learned the hard way that the nannies or au-pairs can be a great addition to the household and to my figure as a housekeeper or a nightmare. In my career, I've met nannies that destroyed vacuums due to sucking all kinds of things but dust or messed up with the laundry and then tried to put the blame on me.

So, at Jessica's, on top of my cleaning duties, I had to oversee organizing the kids' room, putting away all the toys and clothes, helping with the laundry, and naturally keeping up with my schedule because I didn't want to let down my clients.

I struggled to finish in time and include every task in my schedule for this reason; even so, Jessica sometimes left me a note wanting something extra or done differently, which hit me my self-esteem hard every time.

For someone in my position, skeptical about many things, it was difficult to see this behaviour as constructive. However, I tried not to take this personally. It is normal for everyone to prioritize something differently. On the other hand, I have always been treated very kindly and in a friendly environment in Jessica's house and office.

After some time, I discovered that the au-pair would finish her experience with Jessica's family soon, and I was really excited about what would come. The sense of relief was huge. Finally, I realized that the situation would change and that it was worth enduring it all in the end.

I looked forward to being introduced to the next girl in charge of the kids' routine, and that coincided with my own annual leave, meaning that when I got back, I would meet the new live-in au pair!

When I was on holiday and having a great time, I received an email from Jessica's office. With great disbelief, they were firing me, choosing to give my position to another cleaner who worked for their company on another property and who needed extra shifts, according to them.

After this news, of course, I was disappointed and angry and wondered if it was me and if I had done something wrong. Once again, managing rejection was not an easy task, but communication is really important to me, and I wanted honest feedback.

All seemed resolved with a quick chat, and I even had closure by then, but by coincidence, I was scrolling on a site of work advertisements. With great disbelief, a few weeks after that email, I saw a recruitment post for the exact position I held at Jessica's house and office.

Once again, I didn't want to wrap my head around this and jump to any conclusion, so decided to have a confrontation, sending an email to the office. The tone of that email was curious but firm, as to say, "yes, I saw that recruitment ad, and what does this mean?"

Jessica's staff's answer was pre-set and shallow, and they confirmed once more their statement that the other cleaner needed extra shifts, but ultimately, she had decided to seek another employment.

They added a few silly and insignificant details about my work schedule that they weren't happy about to justify themselves, even though they never had a conversation with me about it.

I had given up long ago trying to explain that I, too, have bills, rent and expenses to pay for and groceries to buy. What I don't have is a secure salary each week. I earn what I work hourly for. This means that losing a big account strongly affects my weekly wage, being a sole trader.

Through the years, with difficulty at the beginning, I learned and then perfected the ability to turn negativity into positivity. When something perceived as negative occurs, I use this energy as fuel to create something good. First, meditation helps; of course, the right mindset is crucial. I start with a written list of what was good about that particular situation, what I learned, and in what ways I would feel liberated and a better person without it.

Hence, I also quickly discovered that having closure and moving on once again is fundamental, no matter how hard it is. When you only want to scream, cry and hurt someone but, most importantly, hurt yourself, you need to follow an internal drive and forgive. Not because others deserve your forgiveness but because I deserve my peace of mind.

CHAPTER 6

BE KIND

There is always something so liberating about returning someone's keys. After the anger, guilt, and disappointment, relief and peace of mind take place. Certainly, there are many reasons why the relationship with a client stops, one of the most common ones being a client's moving or relocation. However, seldom, things don't always go as planned, and the keys need to be returned.

While working for Jessica's family, I also had Nick on my working schedule. I'd been contacted by Nick's office regarding a fortnightly cleaning of his office, which was very close to my home, so it worked very well for me. Nick had been working in the sustainability industry, and as usual, we had scheduled a meeting with one of the staff members. The office wasn't big—it consisted of two small offices, around ten desk stations, a kitchenette, a few bathroom cubicles, and a stair. The job would only take a couple of hours. What appealed to me about this company was the innovation, thrive and purpose that they adapted in their teamwork.

I have been lucky enough that the director, Nick, was present in the office and wanted to have a chat with me as well. He looked very easy-going and kind and was impressed with my work ethic. He was also interested in scheduling me to clean his apartment and enquired about my availability.

He had a two-bedroom apartment nearby, so I also accepted this opportunity with pleasure.

In the beginning, at both the office and the director's home, things were going very smoothly; however, soon enough, I started to notice the weird staff turnaround at the office. Obviously, it didn't make any difference to me, but it was nice always seeing the same employees around in case I needed anything or even for a pleasant chat. When I used to come and start my cleaning shift, usually there was still someone around, and within half an hour, they would leave for the day.

The director was very often on business trips, so I was very flexible in cleaning his apartment. However, I barely skipped a clean at his office. Within a few months, though, my invoices started to be processed very late; I even waited for a few months once.

When he was present, Nick started to show regular mood swings, sometimes acting super friendly and sometimes not even greeting me. He started to complain about silly things at his house, such as his laundry being slightly wet from the dryer, even though he knew I could not stay longer due to my tight schedule. Or he kept asking me to work on his many plants on the balcony, even though I told him many times that I don't do anything gardening-related, not even watering the plants because I'm terrible with home plants.

Things went on anyway. The original staff I had known at the beginning had changed by now, and I started to notice that the office became smaller and smaller for the new recruits. As a natural observer, I had started noticing a few signs of a possible moving into a new office, so I started casually investigating with the seniors in the office.

I didn't really get any hint or information about a possible relocation, so I kept doing my usual within my schedule.

Soon enough, it was time for me to take another very needed annual leave, and I had assumed I would return to the same office on my return.

Before boarding my flight from Europe back to Melbourne, I had received an email from the accounts team, from an accountant new to me, advising me that I no longer needed to come and clean that office, as they had relocated (not far from the previous headquarters, I knew that from the paperwork) and they had hired someone else. Nevertheless, I was still welcome to clean the director's apartment.

From a practical point of view, an office is always an easier job than domestic cleaning, so I was far from impressed by this proposal.

In several years working there, I had never missed a workday or arrived late, unless with the due notice obviously, and my reply was very pointed; this behaviour is not considered acceptable after what I had offered throughout my services. Not only had I been ditched without a valid reason or a fair notice, but I had also been kept unaware of the change of circumstances. It wasn't hard to communicate the news in a civil way, even making up an excuse to justify the change of cleaning company; I would get that.

But the cherry on top of the cake, and the proposal to keep cleaning Nick's private house only, after all his mood alterations and weird requests, wasn't really an option. Giving up on the easier part, the office, but keeping the hard part, the private residence. Knowing our worth also means not accepting something that does not seem right, and I couldn't be prouder of my choice.

I didn't have any response from this employee; however, I didn't want to jump to any conclusion. So, I contacted Nick, summarising the happening. I was genuinely thinking that he would apologize, saying that it must have been a mistake from a new accounts team member and that everything could be sorted out. To my surprise, on the contrary, he didn't really mention the office and kept pushing about his apartment, which

I was supposed to still clean regularly. I then cc'd him on the previous emails with the accounts and firmly said that I was not interested in cleaning only his apartment. I only wanted to know the reasons because I wasn't going to accept this disrespectful behaviour.

Then he started writing nonsense, pretending that I didn't really understand English, and so on. There was nothing more for me to say on this regard; my final decision had been to leave this account.

* * *

When I am working, I rarely consider my phone, so I don't follow up to see if I have any texts, let alone answer some calls.

While working for Nick, in the beginning, I had the pleasure of meeting some of his friends. Sometimes, they stayed over at his apartment when he was away, and it was always nice to be introduced to family and friends.

On the last clean, I performed at Nick's house, his sister stayed over, so we exchanged phone numbers. She wanted to have a walk and leave me some freedom to work, so I would contact her when I finished.

And that's how, keeping an eye on my phone in case of her sudden call, on that very morning, I received the first call from a client who would change my entire schedule.

After a very disappointing work experience, I like to take one day off to get the bad vibes out of the system, unwind and go to the dry cleaner. My guilty pleasure is to give some love to my favourite jackets and clothes, just the way I do in my clients' homes.

On a Wednesday morning, I was in the proximity of my local dry cleaner, full of grocery bags and clothes, when I noticed on the pathway that someone had lost a credit card. Straight away, I thought that it must have been the dry cleaner's customer, and I would resolve the matter by handing the card to the staff. Unfortunately, though, they did not have its owner on their system, so they weren't able to help me. I remember being a bit in a rush that day. However, I wanted to do the right thing in trying to get the card back to its owner. I wouldn't want to have something bad on my conscience, such as that credit card going into the wrong hands of someone mischievous. The issuing bank of that card was just around the corner, so I decided to try there. Luckily the staff was very helpful, and they got a hold of their client straight away. They appreciated my gesture, and I could not have been more satisfied and happier about my little detour; someone would probably be happy and relieved because I did the right thing. I really do believe in karma, and what goes around comes around.

The very next day, I set up a meeting with my latest client. Andrew was a friendly and easy-going surgeon in his late thirties, living in one of the coolest suburbs of Melbourne. He had been looking for a regular cleaner with a focus on organizing the house and the laundry.

He also mentioned that every now and then, he would have guests staying over, so I would need to keep an eye on the bed linen laundry. The initial meeting went well; he and his girlfriend were exactly as expected: kind and easy-going. On the day, Andrew told me that I looked skilled and trustworthy and handed me the key to his house.

Trust is a very important point in my work ethic. Being handed the keys on the day of the meeting rarely happens, but it is always a great honour. It meant that my truly genuine work ethic had transpired once again.

Andrew had a tight work schedule and was out of town sometimes, so most of the time, I would let myself in and start my workday. The very first day, I thought I was alone and started by gaining some more confidence of the spacious house and figuring out where all the products and equipment were. I started loading laundry with the bed linens when I heard some noise. I thought Andrew was home, which was a good thing, so if I had any questions, I could ask him right away!

To my surprise, however, another man appeared out of a guest bedroom, wearing the bottom part of his pajamas.

After the first awkwardness, my memory quickly went to my shocking experience with Peter. When dealing with potential male customers, there was always a bit of doubt after my personal experience, also because, in the collective opinion, we believe that cleaning is something mostly women deal with, rather than men.

With great relief, however, this man introduced himself as Andrew's mate. He was friendly and relaxed, and I could sense that this was a totally different situation; he obviously wasn't expecting a housekeeper to be in the house.

I peacefully resumed my chores, and shortly after, the young man also left the house.

* * *

When I get acquainted with someone working in healthcare, I happen to think often about life and death. The latter plays a tricky part in the existence of someone struggling with mental health. It is a very delicate topic to talk about, and I do not have the resources and knowledge to do so.

I remember some of my late teenage years as a pleasant time.

A side of my mother's stability meant that I had an easy ride as well, so I had a semblance of a settled-down life as well. At school, everything went smoothly. I even felt pretty accepted in my class. I had good grades. I was into extracurricular activities such as extra English classes, and I had friendships, a few of which I still maintain today.

My beliefs, mentality, and values of independence, empowerment and gender respect were also understood. It was the era of the early beginnings of social media in the late 2000s, and since I believe that sharing is caring, women from all around the world started to talk about and bringing up the topic of female empowerment and gender equality.

With this new platform of communication, I finally understood that I was not the only one. There was a full community out there with my same values and point of view. This fact contributed to my tranquillity and thrive to be independent.

However, little did I know that my stability was about to get interrupted: in my late teenage years, I lost three friends within less than two years.

Giulia was the pure definition of beauty inside and out. She was enrolled in another class in my same year in high school, and we officially met during a biology project. She was living in my same little town and was always radiant, smiling, and in the company of her numerous friends. Her soul was so pure and kind; there was absolutely no space for negativity, sadness, or falsity in her world. I was extremely blessed to have met her and been in her life. Her energy had been a boost in fighting my demons.

She was also very active in the local town initiatives, so many times, I joined her in helping organize activities.

On the Easter holiday break that year, I learned about a rash on her skin. She kept being happy and joyous, and like her family and friends, she too thought that this rash was only a small irritation, perhaps due to the spring hay fever.

A few days later, the day before returning to school, an extremely acute type of leukemia had taken Giulia away, leaving everyone shocked and the whole school and town in grief.

I will forever be a custodian of the memory of her strength, kindness, radiance, and her big smile.

I met Sara in Italy a couple of years prior in our town's gym. She was around a decade older than me, extremely polite, kind and wise. Her mother was a home visits nurse, and everyone in the neighbourhood respected her professionalism. After noticing that our workouts in the gym were at the same time, Sara and I started chit-chatting and soon became friends in the company of another young woman. The three of us shared gossip and advice and would often meet up outside the gym. Sara also helped and supported me hugely with driving lessons while I was studying for my license.

Sara was overweight and spent lots of time exercising, and I could sense she had a dark past, too. When the time was right, I understood that Sara had been sexually abused by a family friend for most of her childhood and, since then, struggled with bulimia.

I would understand nearly fifteen years later that my childhood had also been filled with subtle abuse. However, it was emotional rather than physical. At the time, I did not know the source of my difficulties. However, I could relate to Sara. There is a distinctive bond that unites victims of mental health conditions.

During the winter, Sara spent the weekend in London with a male friend. On the day they arrived back in Italy, Sara had been declared deceased, officially due to a cardiac arrest. There were many uncertainties regarding Sara's death, and still are to this day. Our friend and I had many doubts about Sara's London trip companion. He had a shady and sinister vibe. Furthermore, the dynamics of her death are still unclear. We would never know if that man had a crucial role, if they had a misunderstanding, or if Sara's body simply stopped working, overwhelmed by her difficult past.

On the day of her funeral, I received her postcard from London in the mail.

When her family and friends were left with a huge loss and grief, I also would have wanted to know her more, to learn more about her past, and try to console her. However, all I have left is her memory filled with courage and braveness, and I will cherish that forever.

Virginia and I had spent the first year of high school in the same class. She was a sweet, introverted and calm girl, very petite but with an extraordinary energy. We bonded immediately and started our friendship; we were both quiet and shy girls, an only child, and we liked the same music and school subjects. The following year, Virginia changed class, but we were in the same school, so we were in touch every day, and we often saw each other in our spare time. I remember how we went to visit Venice one day, often going to the beach together during summertime or shopping.

Through the years, I have seen my friend Virginia blossom into a very beautiful young woman, and she started to become very popular and contended for by some boys. In that same period, she sadly announced her parent's separation. It was clear that Virginia was very upset about her parents splitting, which would take a big toll on her.

Soon afterward, Virginia tried to take her own life by ingesting a mix of pills. Luckily, her mother noticed her lying senseless on the floor and promptly called an ambulance. The doctors arrived in time to save my friend's life.

After this incident, Virginia was clearly unstable and upset, still grieving her parents' separation. She had entered an unhealthy pattern and started a relationship with a guy who was only bad news. I also knew the boy from our school: he was a typically arrogant, entitled, and popular young man. In my opinion, he had nothing to share with Virginia, a girl I knew as kind, sweet, caring, and loyal.

As expected, this boy soon started treating her badly, cheating on her, making her jealous, and submitting her to psychological violence.

I lived close to my summertime job when I learned about Virginia's death in a car accident. In that moment, I only remember the blur; I was in the hall of the apartment complex I had been living in when the landlords saw me, clearly in shock, and came to the rescue, making me lie down and giving me a calming pill.

The car crash occurred the evening before when Virginia's boyfriend was driving his car, with another person in the passenger seat and my friend lying down in the back seat. He lost control of the car and hit a tree. In the impact,

Virginia broke her neck, instantly losing her life.

The driver and the other passenger didn't get a scratch from the collision, and the driver had never taken any responsibility for his actions. He was the son of the emergency room primary of the town, and to my knowledge, no alcohol or drug test was conducted after the crash.

On the first encounter with death, my friend Virginia had a guardian angel that saved her, but perhaps destiny had other plans for this sweet and caring young soul.

I carry the legacy of these three extraordinary women with me and cherish all the memories we built together.

The aftermath was pretty hard on me. I have always been a lone wolf and had difficulty building rapport, so losing not one or two but three precious friends left me scarred.

I started, once again, asking myself why this all kept happening to me. When will enough be enough, and have I not endured plenty of traumatic events for a woman who was not even twenty years old? I started thinking about a curse on myself, that I had been a link between these three friends who did not know each another.

Today more than ever, I want to speak up about the importance of mental health. If seeking professional mental health was not seen as taboo, two of my friends might still be alive today because they would have been able to seek treatment to help them deal with their mental health issues.

Yes, that physical abuse is something possible to overcome. Yes, we might feel vulnerable after our parents split and the family dynamics change, but it is possible to heal with the right guidance.

I did not know how to find that guidance then, after losing my friends, and once again, little did I know about what was going to happen in my near future.

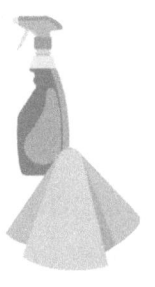

CHAPTER 7

BAD BLOOD

I don't believe that we need to condone everything because of blood relations. If a certain relationship is toxic, it is best to do everything to resolve the problems or tensions. However, if this is not possible, we need to cut all the ties and not be held back just because of a family relation. It's either letting go or being dragged.

Communication is very important in every aspect of life, and I have learned this the hard way. No one will read our minds or assume what is going on in our heads. So, in order to live a fulfilled life, we must ask that question, express our feelings and define our expectations.

For my well-being and mental health, I made the decision not to have any connection or communication with my birth mother several years ago.

On the other hand, my father sadly passed away more than a decade ago, shortly after losing my three beloved friends. I didn't realize how much I was grieving, and I embarked on another wave of depression. I was not ready, though, for the biggest suffering I would ever have to experience: a loss of a parent due to a maleficent illness.

Exactly two months before my father's sudden death, by coincidence, I had been spending a weekend in Venice. I met a group of friends only the week prior at a summer garden party. They asked me to join them on this Erasmus trip, organized for the Italian and international students but also open to outsiders. This was a typical experience you only do in the early twenties, so I accepted the invitation with pleasure and, surprisingly, without a drop of worry.

The organized accommodation was a youth hostel, a massive and charming Venetian-style old red brick building facing San Marco square. The ground floor displayed the check-in and information desks, the breakfast hall, and a generous-sized lounge. The upper floors' interiors featured spacious rooms, separated by gender, each containing around ten beds and a huge bathroom at every floor's end. Getting ready and having a shower every day while overlooking San Marco's campanile is still pleasantly stuck in my mind.

The hostel was located on an island, one of the many composing the town of Venice, facing the main square, and it was about twenty minutes on a ferry trip to the town's main district.

That weekend, I had the best time, met many students from different countries, and practiced my Spanish and English with my new acquaintances. We had a sangria party, courtesy of the Iberian students, walked through the charming Venetian little lanes called *calles*, admired the distinctive canals, went to the casino, and had many happy hours— activities that every teenager should have in their youth. One evening, a few other girls and I even accepted a lift on a boat from a strange group of young men: we were so content and carefree and enjoyed the experience of a night ride, and I realized later that something like that would be impossible to embark on nowadays.

When I told my parents about my unforgettable weekend, my dad confided to me that the hostel we had stayed at a few decades prior had been the boarding school he was enrolled in. During the post-war times, it was normal to send teenage children to study away from home in these humble mansions that used to be a place for school education.

Soon after, I understood this fact as a sign; destiny brought me to the same hostel where my dad studied many years ago, right before saying farewell to him.

I will forever treasure the time spent with my dad and the important life lessons I have learned, such as being responsible, ambitious, loyal and respectful.

Nevertheless, my father's passing left a turmoil of chaos, anger, and greed linked to his will. Many relatives with whom I had no relationships created dramas just to get their hands on anything, but most importantly, to not let my mother or me inherit the family's estate.

After more than twenty years, we were still seen as outsiders rather than my dad's beloved family.

This was another strong hit on my trust issues and self-esteem. At the time, I was only a twenty-year-old girl. The only problems I wanted to have been how to dress up to go out or if I should go on that date, certainly not feeling so little and alone in this crazy world, arguing with third-grade entitled cousins, or having to learn a notary's dictionary.

The aftermath was filled with sadness, animosity among relatives, being forced to take antidepressant pills against my will and a huge sense of emptiness.

Whilst I am not comfortable entering into the details of the circumstances that led me to be forced to take medication without my consent, I can gladly say that the family's estate matters were resolved peacefully, thanks to the precision of all the relevant paperwork.

* * *

Professionally speaking, the family feud reminded me of another peculiar yet unfortunate work experience.

I have never considered myself a good person, but I haven't considered myself a bad person either for most of my life. That doesn't mean that I don't deserve respect as a person and as a working woman.

I normally seek and source my clientele privately, without any broker or intermediate ways. I want to deal with, present, and talk with a potential client personally. However, in my career, it had happened that, mostly out of curiosity, I would apply for a position on an app or recruiting site, only to find out that there is an agency in between.

A recruitment agency works as a broker between those who are looking to hire someone, in my case a housekeeper, and the candidates who would apply for the advertisement.

My curriculum and experience normally fit perfectly for these kinds of advertisements. On the other side of these advertisements are usually very rich people, the so-called high-profile personalities.

Every time, though, I promised myself to hold on from proceeding in the recruitment process, and every time that I didn't listen to my principles, I regretted my choice.

So, one day, I applied for a cleaning job based in Melbourne, which looked like an ideal opportunity for my portfolio from the advertisement.

Jane from the recruitment agency replied to my application within a few hours, complimenting me for my experience, saying that I was a good candidate and that she was going to set up a meeting with Anna, her client. We then exchanged some emails back and forth about the little details, some of them quite annoying such as the request for my personal pictures: my job doesn't involve modelling or such, so I didn't really get why they wanted me to send photos of my appearance.

During the long phone calls, I was told about some details of the position or the house but could sense that this client was very indecisive and insecure. What I should wear both during the interview and during my potential workdays was strongly suggested: corporate apparel for the interview without high heels and a smart black outfit at work. I politely tried to explain that I knew how to dress for an interview and definitely didn't need to be uncomfortable in high heels (Jane was sure of the fact that high heels for an interview equals less willingness to work hard, and although I had a lot to say on this topic, I just agreed).

Furthermore, I have noticed that when I am working in my uniform, I tend to look way younger than my actual age, and many times in recent years, I have been mistaken for a teenager. Hence, many people thought I was too young to know certain rules of common sense or acknowledge that I was a professional cleaner and not a student picking up random jobs to make ends meet.

However, there was a bit of tension regarding my potential workdays at Anna's. At work, I always wear my uniform, with my company's logo, a pair of comfortable pants, and sneakers. With the usual monologue full of fancy words, Jane told me that this would not be possible at Anna's residence because the uniform represents my company as an external party, and they wanted someone to be basically in line with the prestige of their home, wearing smart black pants, T-shirt and shoes.

I didn't agree, but the position interested me; even though these little details had nearly put me off, I was willing to try it instead of having regrets.

Anna's family, though, didn't want a cleaner; they wanted a housekeeper. When Jane had asked me why I promoted myself as a cleaning lady instead of a housekeeper, I simply told her that the latter word meant something more intimidating, inclusive, and high-end for my potential middle-class clientele, and indeed this was the case.

Anna was an elegant, polite, but severe-looking woman in her mid-to-late forties. She was well dressed in comfortable and casual but high-end clothes, which you recognize as luxury brands only in a wealthy setting. Despite her charming and unusual background, she had a strong American accent. Her manners were classy but wary, giving me the impression of always being alert.

The meeting with Anna had been set for the next day, and as expected, it was textbook, full of the usual questions that only recruiters ask, to which you would only give one of those general answers that meant everything and nothing at the same time.

That meet and greet didn't really leave me satisfied, as I like to set up the tone regarding the type of client I'm talking to as this creates a very personal yet informal situation. On top of that, I noticed that some details of Jane's version of the job didn't really match, for example, I'd been told that in the mansion there would be many stairs and I'd been asked if I were comfortable and fit for that; however, I didn't see one single step in that house. Or that seldom I would have to work in the afternoons or early evenings on demand, according to my availability, and again Anna didn't mention this particular.

Finally, we also discussed my salary, and Anna offered me straight away $10 above my hourly rate. Everyone being told this would probably be extremely happy, but I knew there was a catch. There are people so poor out there that the only thing they own is money.

Working for Anna's was one of my most humiliating work experiences, and I have never felt treated so low.

Their mansion was a lovely single-storey large Victorian house, completely renovated, combining a classic style with a modern twist inside. The house was very tidy and spotless. My shifts were twice per week in order to maintain that standard. Being Italian, I recognized straight away all the beautiful and expensive features of the house, such as a high-end Scavolini kitchen, Carrara marble in the bathrooms, imported wooden floors, and a huge laundry room complete with Miele appliances. Some of the decors in the house were ornamental—Fornasetti plates, Jo Malone big candles in nearly every room, and Murano glass vases. Something peculiar that I noticed was that Anna had a lock on every wardrobe drawer.

I believe that Anna was very satisfied with my services workwise. She recognized my passion, expertise and efforts in my job. She was also very pleased when I introduced her to my favourite brand of cleaning products, and she liked them so much that she stocked her laundry with months' worth of supplies.

However, having struggled with acceptance, trust and low self-esteem myself, I could truly understand how Anna felt insecure. Money doesn't solve all problems, and I really felt like I was a pet she could mistreat.

She constantly checked on me, wandering around the house pretending to do something, but in reality, making sure I was continuing my work or checking what product I was using. When I walked from one room to another, she even got scared of my presence, even though she knew I was nearby. She always gave me feedback on how to do my job or the order in which I should do it; sometimes, I even tried to explain my professional point of view, but sometimes I just gave up and listened. So many little things put together made me feel small compared to their wealth and majesty.

In every bathroom, expensive Aesop hand wash and creams were displayed, yet the hand soap was different in the tiny guest powder room I was allowed to use. Even though I always carried with me my reusable water flask, she insisted every time on offering me a mainstream plastic bottle of water while she set out a San Pellegrino sparkling water for herself.

The more she made those remarks, the more she felt superior. The more she paid me above the average, the more she thought she could tell someone hired what to do.

After a few times, we mutually decided that I was definitely not the right housekeeper for Anna's household. On the last day, we didn't agree on something minor, and how I was treated didn't suit me. If you're not able to trust anyone but yourself, you shouldn't hire anyone in the first place. All the assurances in the world, references, and background checks won't give you any peace if this is not found within ourselves.

I have never been impressed by wealth and money. I am impressed by clean manners, a good heart, kindness, and positive energy. I am certain that not all wealthy people are pretentious and superior to others, just as I don't believe all normal people are caring and good-hearted.

* * *

I didn't discourage myself after the experience with Anna. On the contrary, it fuelled me to do better, to be better, and to increase my boundaries.

At this stage in my career, I wanted more. Now, I wanted that missing client who made the difference, someone who was eager to have a good cleaning lady and would speak highly of her to their circle.

Shortly after my experience at Anna's, on a warm and lovely summer afternoon, Jasmine contacted me for the first time. She and her husband were looking for a weekly clean in the most prestigious suburb of Melbourne.

They had just bought their home, which was a superb mansion previously owned by an artist. References to 70's architecture were everywhere, and the layout reminded me of a Stanley Kubrick movie.

The living area was in the middle of the house, and two side wings contained all the rooms, bathrooms, living areas, and the kitchen. Opposite the main living room, there was a lovely bar, in which, if you were invited to, you would only order a drink such as an old- fashioned.

The job was really inspiring and relatively easy because Jasmine had been planning some minor renovations and repainting of the walls. Furthermore, she mentioned that she wanted to introduce me to her mum's and brother's houses, both located in the neighbourhood. I was really impressed and blown away by this proposal. In fact, a few weeks later, I even got to meet the property manager of the family estates, and he congratulated me on my work. He said he heard impressive feedback about me, both for my skills and discretion.

Soon enough, I learned that the family had the full-time help of a butler, a situation that had never happened in my career. When I started to clean Jasmine's mum's and brother's houses occasionally, my role was to lighten up the butler's duties and support him while he was dealing with other tasks. My allocated main duties were the bathrooms, which happened to be one of my favourite tasks.

Throughout the mansions, the bathrooms were among the most luxurious I have ever seen. In the master bedroom, there were even two bathrooms, for her and for him, and the dimensions of those rooms were like an average house's bedroom rather than a bathroom. All the materials were imported and only of the highest standard available, and they even had a bidet in each bathroom. As an Italian, this made me proud: a bidet is a bowl, usually next to the toilet and similar in shape to it, which is used to wash the intimate parts of the body and is present in every household in Italy.

Every now and then, the butler checked on me to see if I was okay or needed anything, as the mansions were so big, it was easy to get lost!

One of the first times, I asked him what he thought of my work on a particular bathroom to be sure it was the standard requested by the clients. Jokingly, he said that I was really the queen of all the shower screens, and, with great pleasure, this would be my unofficial alias from that moment on.

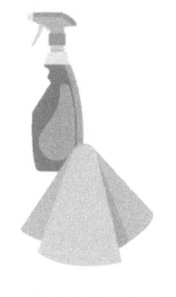

CHAPTER 8

ANGELS

Happiness: how many times do we say this word every day, and how often do we feel truly happy about something that happened to us? Despite it being one of the most common feelings, I don't remember being truly happy until my early twenties, precisely when I met my husband.

When you're in the cycle of depression and instability since childhood, it's really hard to know the difference between what is considered normal and what is not, what should bring you good emotions, and what not. Furthermore, when one or both of your parents cannot see who needs to seek professional help first to get the family in a better place, you just give up on happiness. You start to become your own parent in a way.

You only know that sad side of life, it is like a filter, and you live with it and through it.

As a little kid, I remember visiting many psychologists, always by myself and every time without any success. I did not persevere. I did not feel comfortable or supported, and the base problem was that I was not the problem. In fact, the family dynamics I was living in were not healthy.

Most times when I visited a child psychologist, I only went there for the first session, so it was hard, if not impossible, to have a clear picture and attribute the right therapy for my case.

It took me two decades to understand that I was not the issue, that I deserved to be happy, and that it is okay if I didn't get the right guidance in life. Sometimes things happen for the best, and by the time I became a grown-up woman, I had found my way; that cycle had ended for me when I started my journey to become a person capable of being happy and accepting happiness.

Workwise, nearly all my clients have often told me how happy and positive I've always looked, and this has always filled my heart. Creating my own business certainly brought many joyful and positive moments. I always like to bring good energy with me, and it took me years to learn that it doesn't matter what happens in life; it is the way we react to things that counts. Sometimes it is hard to stay calm, everyone has bad moments in life, but I pledged this to be one of my mantras.

* * *

I am very lucky that I get to choose whom I want to work for. Sometimes you find clients with whom you're particularly on the same page and have a special bond with. The key, as usual, is being friendly without being a friend and being at service without being too present.

After the big wave of the COVID-19 pandemic and the series of lockdowns in Melbourne had ended, I experienced the period with the most job requests ever. I didn't place any advertisements, but somehow the request from both private clients and companies kept coming. Some of them had my contact already in their database; some had my details through mutual contacts. The messages of work proposals were up to five or six per day. The limited availability of my agenda, driven by the thrive of coming back to do my job after many restrictions across the city of Melbourne, had been prioritized by the location and length of the job.

There are two types of clients: the ones who treat you as a cleaner and the ones who treat you as a person.

I was very glad that Greg fitted my schedule perfectly and that he contacted me just in time. Since the first meeting, I understood how kind, respectful, and good-hearted Greg was. He was an engineer and had been living, back then, with two lovely, friendly, beautiful inside and out female housemates. They all also shared their townhouse with a cute little dog and two adorable cats. I consider myself a cat person, so saying that I fell in love with their felines is an understatement! Everyone knows that cats are usually independent, cold, and sometimes not so friendly, but Greg's cats were the complete opposite: sweet, cuddly, loving and always up for playtime. Since day one, these feline sisters simply became known as the Angels.

Needless to say, I started working for Greg, and I was so glad, in the first place, because I was finally able to do the job I love again after so many months of hard lockdowns, and secondly, because the household was such fun, relaxed, and full of furry friends! I remember always staying a bit longer than the agreed time and having lots of play with the pets and bringing them some very appreciated treats every now and then.

After some months, Greg's housemates had moved out to another home, and he needed to travel to visit some relatives, so it came naturally for him to ask me to look after the Angels while he was away. I was so happy and honoured with the proposal and couldn't say no, so my husband and I hosted his cats for a few months. We remember those times with so much joy and positivity. The Angels are the cuddliest and most easy-going cats ever! We played, let them cuddle us, and created many memories and funny challenges for them.

When Greg returned from his trips, we were so sad at the idea of returning the cats to him; the house would seem so empty without them! However, he asked if we would be interested in adopting the Angels permanently, and with great joy, we accepted the offer, and the Angels are still part of our family.

To this date, I still help Greg's household and clean his home. I update him regularly about the cats when he is out of town and have met some of his relatives and his lovely parents, who welcomed me so warmly and every time spoiled me with some delicacies of their home country.

I always say that when I meet a client's parents, they are always a more mature and experienced version of their children, and this couldn't be truer about Greg's family.

I can't say the same about my love for dogs, as I am not a huge fan of them. Melbourne happens to be one of the most dog-friendly cities in the world, and when dealing with a new customer, it is always a delicate topic. I want to respect everyone's home environment but also set up some boundaries. I am not really bothered with small dogs; they are usually the nice, fluffy, and calm ones. I feel uncomfortable around big, scary-looking ones, which are also the most popular. These breeds seem to be the most energetic and smelly, and they keep jumping on everyone.

Naturally, it should be a potential client's duty to let the housekeeper know about the presence of any pet in the house and enquire whether it could be an issue, but in my career, this only happened once or twice. I understand that probably the pet owners do not see their dogs as an issue. When my real estate agency, or a particular technician, contacts me for any maintenance job to fix something in my house, on every occasion, I have been asked if there are dogs or relevant big pets on the property. This means that I am not the only one having issues with safety or potentially being uncomfortable around certain animals. Once again, there is no school for common sense.

A very clear example is when I worked briefly at Scott's house. He and his partner lived in a cute ground-floor apartment in the inner city with two bedrooms, two bathrooms, and a small outdoor area.

They were both full-time professionals, so they were home mostly in the evenings, and their apartment was not too bad to clean; it was a pretty straightforward job. Most of the time, the vacuum had been neglected, and the filter was dirty, so making it work properly was standard procedure in most first cleans.

During my first clean, however, I was surprised to see an angry-looking dog in their apartment, which was neither present nor mentioned during the initial meeting. I was uncomfortable around it and asked if they could put it in the outdoor area, stating that I am not really a dog person. They were clearly shocked by this reaction and also seemed slightly offended.

After that and before leaving for work, they said that their idea was that when I would come to clean their home fortnightly, it was my duty to put the dog from inside the apartment to the outside area to clean.

I am still unsure if my face let slip my reaction, but with all the politeness in me, I answered that this would not happen. Furthermore, a large dog is something that should be stated before hiring a professional, let alone dealing with it.

As mentioned earlier, and as mentioned in all my work advertisements, I wasn't dealing with short rentals, or Airbnb cleans. I decided to give it another go at Scott's house after they promised me to remove their dog on the day of the cleaning. The next time I scheduled their cleaning, they left me the keys to the apartment in the mailbox, as usual. When I opened the door, however, I was inundated by a terrible smell, something so nauseating I had never experienced before and was shocked to see a family of total strangers sitting in the living room. They didn't seem to be bothered by my presence, looked like tourists, and did not speak a word of English.

Straight away, I texted Scott to check and ask about what was going on.

Without using the word "Airbnb," he explained that this was indeed a short-term rental, and I would have to do the usual tasks, plus changing the bed linen. I also told him about the unbearable smell in his apartment; it felt like an indoor landfill that hadn't been opened for fresh air in months and asked if he remembered that I don't deal with short-term rental cleans.

He simply left me instructions regarding the bed linens that needed to be changed and to report him if I saw anything weird or damaged in the house.

I had trouble, though, finding the right sheets for the beds. After sorting out every bed set, I had seen, I decided to let it go, as my time was nearly up, and my schedule had other jobs that day. I could not do anything more if the right size of bed linen were not present in the storage unit. I did not text a message to Scott about the bed linen. In my experience, it would only be a waste of time: I would tell him my version of being in his house, and he would say his, being away from home, and we wouldn't resolve anything with the "it's not here, yes, it is there" method.

I did not leave a note about the bed linen, and I believe Scott was not pleased about that, and he didn't even bother to text me or let me know not to come anymore. Lastly, changing the beds was not even part of my duties agreed with the client.

I am not for everybody; I am aware of that, and in fact, I had no real interest in that job. The dog situation and making me clean for an

Airbnb (hence possibly charging more money for the cleaning to his guests but paying me my regular rate) had been enough for me to move on happily.

Often people ask me what the most disgusting things are that I have seen in my job, somehow assuming it would be related to bathroom chores, but partly, they are far from wrong. My personal chart about what I am really repelled about is: used condoms found randomly around the house (yes, people do not always dispose of them properly in the rubbish bin), remains of food in the kitchen sink, and toilets not flushed.

One of the messiest houses I have ever worked in was an on-demand spring clean opportunity found through mutual contacts. It was the residence of five professionals in the construction industry, and they had trouble finding a housekeeper, so as a favour on a one-off basis, I accepted the offer.

The money was generous, and it would have been a long day of work.

Saying that the house had not been cleaned in months would be an understatement; upon entry, the smell of untidiness, dirty clothes, and stale food was very strong, and I was already prepared for a day of hard work.

The bedrooms were very pretty messy and dusty, and the bed lines would have to be changed. I was not able to do all the laundry, however, because when there is no dryer, I am only able to wash one or two loads.

The two bathrooms featured dirty toilets that were not flushed, greasy sinks and mirrors, and the floors were a coat of soap and long hair.

The kitchen bench was full of take-away food containers, most of them still with remains of food from days ago, and the stove was an outburst of sauces and stains; it was impossible to see the steel grey colour of the appliance. All the cabinets had different spots, there were empty beer and wine bottles around the living area, and the bins were extremely full. The payment agreed upon was pretty good; however, I did not charge an extra fee due to the horrid state of the place.

Overall, without a doubt, among the most annoying tasks I often performed was sorting out the bins.

In Melbourne, in most city councils, there are three different bins: general waste, recycling, and organic green waste.

Sometimes the waste is not disposed of properly, to begin with. Nevertheless, generally the bins in the houses many times were so full, and the rubbish bag was so crammed that every time they would just be buried by the extra rubbish that blocked the lid from being closed. The result was a bag too heavy, and it was nearly impossible to take the bag out. The base of the bin had food and a mess on the lid. This sequence happened most of the time because people did not change the rubbish bag in time, apparently waiting for a supernatural power to perform this task in between my cleaning sessions.

Among the unique things I have seen in my career were guns and confidential drafts of important documents. However, a spicier secret to keep for a housekeeper had been the discovery of an affair of someone married I used to work for. I prefer not to disclose the circumstances of how I learned about the cheating. Once again, discretion and open-mindedness are fundamental in my career.

I do not know how that particular affair had proceeded then, nor am I able to say if the partner had to find out about that, but surely it was not in my place to hint or say anything. Once again, I am happy as long as I am not involved.

On the other hand, the most disrespectful meet and greet I have ever experienced was with a family of professionals, both working as doctors and living in a spacious house in a lovely suburb.

After the usual initial chitchat and tour of their home, which went very well, they showed me the feature of their traditional kitchen following a kosher regime: in a kosher kitchen, the items used for preparing and serving meat and dairy must be separated. Hence, there must be two sets of utensils, pots, pans, plates, and silverware for meat, poultry, and dairy foods.

For that reason, appliances often come double: two refrigerators, two cooking ranges, sinks, dishwashers, and so on. So, during my cleaning session, I would have to adhere to this method and use two different cloths to clean the kitchens and all the surfaces.

Being an accepting and unbiased person and professional, I replied that it was not a problem and that I may need some guidance the first time in order to satisfy my client's standard, being that was my very first experience.

When the couple asked me about my rate, and I answered, their reaction was, "Oh, that is a lot of money!"

The rate I had been charging was in line for a professional cleaner operating as a sole trader, but considering my company's insurance, the expenses of products, and fuel, I might have been even on the less expensive side of pay grade. Furthermore, I did not charge them a premium for their unusual work request, which lots of other professionals fairly applied.

With all the politeness and patience, I had in me, I thanked them for their time and proceeded to the exit door. They also hinted that they paid the previous cleaning lady a rate that was under the legal wage, let alone the rate considered lawful for a sole trader working with an Australian Business Number.

Nevertheless, it was not my place to explain and justify my price list. If someone seems not respectful of my professionalism, then it is not worth my attention and time.

I would like to remark that I do not have any judgment or bias whatsoever regarding any nationality, social status, gender, religion, or political standing. I learned relatively early on that these do not define if we are a good or a bad person, respectful or disrespectful.

* * *

Lastly, one of the weirdest experiences would be cleaning up after a sex party held in the house of a regular client. On that occasion, I learned that it is possible to rent out a particular charming property to a certain sex club. There could be different night themes, and at that specific time, it was related to Japanese geishas.

I had no idea about that the event that had taken place, and when I arrived on the day of the cleaning, I was overwhelmed by an oriental setup with cute umbrellas and sensually written Japanese words.

Most of the job would have been tidying up the living area, where refreshments and meet-ups were held.

All the bed linens of the house would have to be changed, and the rooms cleared up, given that whoever wished to explore another participant intimately had to do that in the bedrooms but with the doors open. There were, in fact, many rules written upon entry in every room and bathroom. The first rule was to be extremely discreet, and phone usage for interaction was banned.

Privacy regarding the identities of the participants was paramount, and it was absolutely prohibited to take photos and videos, as well as use any kind of drug. Drinking alcohol was not recommended, or at least not in abundance, as every participant must stay sober, consent to, and be in control of their actions. Another rule was to use protection during sexual intercourse.

Lastly, the organizers were always checking on the participants, even during the intimate moments, to check that everything was proceeding smoothly and consensually, hence the rule of keeping every door open at any time. I knew all these rules because they were written on a page and put on every door in the house.

Yet again, in my job, the first principle is the be considerate and open-minded, and I had absolutely no judgment regarding this work experience. As long as whoever joins these parties is conscious of their actions, it is not in my expertise to say what is right or wrong.

From my professional perspective, it was a fairly easy job, and I sent the invoice to the event organizers.

CHAPTER 9

FEAR OF ADDICTION OR ADDICTION TO FEAR?

We all have fears; it is a natural part of being human and often a way to react to the unknown. Personally, all my fears disappeared a few years ago, on the day I found out I was pregnant with my first son.

For a big part of my life, however, one of my fears was abandonment.

Although it is not an official phobia, the fear of abandonment is a form of anxiety and arguably one of the most common and damaging fears. People with a fear of abandonment may display behaviours and patterns that affect their relationships. Our behaviours and actions in current relationships are all thought to be the result of old fears and learned concepts that take place in childhood.

Indeed, my fear started when I did not get the right nurture as a little kid and intensified with the lack of a united family. I was never asked how my day was returning from school, shown any interest in my schedule and extracurricular activities, or shown any engagement in family assemblies.

My fear of abandonment intensified during my teenage years, after many years of neglected emotions, lack of genuine care from my family, and the passing away of my precious friends, hence the difficulty in building further relationships.

Nevertheless, by the time my relationship with my latest regular clients ended, I had already started my journey to well-being. I had been seeing a therapist regularly, and the fear of abandonment was among the first ones to be resolved.

I remember noticing these little details, how my mindset was different, how the new version of myself reacted differently to these minor changes in life, compared to the old me, who would overthink, picture the worst scenario, and blame only herself for not being enough.

For instance, Jasmine's family had businesses and enterprises overseas, so frequently, the whole family would move for several months at a time, leaving me with a huge work gap in my schedule. Being a sole trader, it was a problem for me, given that a big part of my schedule would be on hold, and it wouldn't have been fair to find another work solution for only a few months. Considering these factors, it was understandable that I would look at different and more permanent work opportunities.

I am still in touch with Jasmine. We parted on excellent terms, and sometimes I even helped her with a few house chores on an occasional basis.

A fear, however, that had been way more difficult to overcome was the fear of spiders. This is also a very common phobia, and it is still not clear what the origin of it is. Some experts say that we are all born with this fear; others believe that this fear comes from actually being bitten by a spider in tender years, and other researchers embrace the theory of evolutionary origins.

Surely, in me, this fear loomed in my elementary school years because, as a child, during my Russian summer breaks, I remember being happy and careless during our weekends at the family Dacha. Here, with all the greenery, trees, and simply made houses, naturally lived and existed all kinds of little insects.

Australia is a country famous for its massive and poisonous spiders, such as the funnel web, redback, or trapdoor. Luckily these wild creatures are to be found mostly outside the big cities and usually in humid places, immersed in the rich Australian nature. However, in the rainiest and most humid cities like Sydney, redbacks have made their way into houses and garages.

Melbourne's climate is the complete opposite: cold in wintertime and not that humid. However, I have had my share of big scares in my workplace due to spiders.

I had been working for a few months at Chloe's house, a charming townhouse in a lovely inner-city suburb, for a few months when I noticed that on the day of our scheduled clean, the weather had been crazy:

an end-of-summer thunderstorm day with very high humidity. I am a cold-weather kind of person, so my only concern on really warm days was that it would be too hot to work. Where I work the most in my clients' houses, in the bathrooms, and in the kitchens, there is no direct air conditioning normally.

The job at Chloe's house was easy. Her family was really tidy, minimal and organized, which is the best scenario for a cleaner, and my duty was basically maintenance. On that particular day, I had nearly finished. I was disassembling their vacuum and organizing the bucket with the mop when I noticed that something was off. On one of the high-ceiling corners of Chloe's living room, there was a massive spider—a huntsman. It was the biggest I have ever seen, bigger than a human's hand when spread out. A huntsman is one of Australia's scariest and biggest spiders, despite being harmless and not poisonous (personal suggestion: if you do not know what a huntsman spider looks like and are afraid of spiders, please do not Google it!).

Straight away, I froze, and I think I stayed like that for a minute, trying not to overreact but clearly having a panic attack. As usual, I was alone at Chloe's house, and my only reassurance was that the spider did not move; it remained in the ceiling corner.

Luckily, the house had a back door to a little backyard, so straight away, I went outside and tried to breathe. It was a hot day for a panic attack; breathing was difficult, my heart was beating fast, and I was very dizzy. I managed to call Chloe and explain the situation, asking if someone would be home soon or if she had someone trusted in the area who could help me and remove the spider. Unfortunately, she did not, and everyone would return home later on, so we both agreed that if I felt uncomfortable, it was probably better for me to leave from the back door and call it a day, given that I had also nearly finished my chores. I gathered my products and my purse, which fortunately were close to the back exit, and left the house from the backyard.

This was the only time when I didn't finish a job. I was very grateful, however, that my client was very understanding and reassuring. Having lived overseas, she also understood that spiders in Australia could be intimidating.

I continued working for Chloe and her family for some more time before they relocated and moved to another property.

* * *

Another totally different thing Melbourne is famous for is the usage of recreational drugs, particularly cocaine. Having worked in the intimacy of people's houses, I saw many times hidden sachets of white powder, and seldom even not that hidden, but very well exposed on a fancy plate after a successful party.

After years in the profession, it's not that hard to understand who a user might be. First of all, the location and the lifestyle play a crucial role, and secondly, the body signs always give a clue. Having a certain boost of energy, seeming unstoppable, and having bright eyes with dilated pupils is the usual pattern for a cocaine user. After these first clues, in a few months' time, there were dentist's bills on the desk and Viagra pills in the bathroom cabinet.

In my job, it is essential not to be judgemental, and despite personally not being tempted by anything that might give me any addictions, I always say that I am happy with everything as long as I am not involved.

Every now and then, I happened to help my most loyal clients with on-demand tasks. I remember a case when I helped organize a moving out for a client who had not been in Melbourne due to a work project. Their lease had expired, and that property was not available anymore, so my clients had to vacate the property, however, their being out of town had complicated the job.

Being a lover of organization, I happily took over the task. For the next few days, my job was to deal with the removal employees, speak with their manager about all the details, and be present with the keys to the property.

I also looked around the house for cash and small precious things in case they got lost in the big moving boxes. So, as agreed, I held onto a wallet and some of my client's belongings for some time. When the time to meet my clients and give back their precious items arrived, by coincidence, I noticed that for this whole time, I held a few sachets of white powder in that particular wallet, among the other objects, without my knowledge.

While I was in Russia during my childhood, the memory of an experience that stuck with me was my first testimony on how brutal drugs are.

An acquaintance of my mother, a classy and wealthy woman, had been dating someone in that period in the late 1990s. My mother had never met that man, but her friend, an ambitious entrepreneur, told my mother that her partner was a man of good family and values.

One day, this friend called my mother, telling her that an emergency had just happened and asking her to come straight to her residence.

The entrepreneur was living in a spacious apartment that originally had been two different adjacent flats, which she had bought and united into one larger residence.

The apartment, located in a prestigious area of Volgograd, featured a large living area, in big contrast with the traditional tiny Russian flats constructed during the Soviet era, which was modern and unconventional for that time period.

My mother did not know the nature of the emergency from the phone call and arrived quickly to assist her friend with me, at that time around a ten-year-old child.

The revelation left my mother speechless: the female friend not only had just learned that the man she had been dating was a drug addict, but he had just passed away due to an overdose in her freshly renovated bathroom. Straight away, I was sent to the caring neighbours; thankfully, the friend had a kind and understanding elderly couple living next door who looked after me for a few hours.

As a little kid, luckily, I did not realize what was happening, and do not remember being shocked or emotionally affected by that episode; amid that situation, my mother had tried not to expose me to that dramatic event. She did not disclose any additional information; however, many years later, she reported what a nasty situation it had been and how messy her poor friend's new bathroom had been left in.

When I was a teenager in Italy, I was in a relatively good place and found a weekend job in public relations for a local disco club. I had been going to that discotheque already and I had many acquaintances going there as well as schoolmates, so it was pleasant to go a step further and be a part of the organization.

The main duty of the public relations staff was to promote the events and DJ sets held by that club. Every Saturday, the first step was to collect the promotional flyers for the next event and, during the week, distribute them in certain areas such as school boards, local cafes and shops, as well as hand them to clubgoers' friends. Every PR had a designated area where to distribute their share of pamphlets, agreed upon with the supervisors. It often happened to see other PR's bulletins in a place or coffee shop far from their assigned area, of course, but it was a matter diligently controlled by the area supervisors. Like in every field in life, shortcuts do not bring anything, and it had been a good lesson about those who did not follow the rules.

Furthermore, every PR had its own guest list, usually formed by friends, and the advantage of being on the list was, for instance, a reduction in the entry fee or a complimentary drink.

Every Saturday, the staff were handed an envelope with the payment: it was not an extraordinary amount, but it was a reasonable coffee change for a teenager.

During this experience, I learned how many drugs exist and circulate in the nightlife world. I have seen everything, from wild behaviour due to very popular pills, to hopeless girls doing anything for a line as well as the infamous "rape pills" put in the drinks of unfortunate and non-consenting young women. Personally, however, I was never interested in any kind of drugs circulating in the clubs, perhaps because I had already been exposed to pharmaceutical antidepressant drugs in my family, administered without my consent.

Contrary, and I am still far from proud of this fact, I preferred to drown my worries and problems in alcohol. My luck, however, had been limiting my drinking while working at the discotheque, especially after what I had seen weekly. Hence, I was used to ordering mostly bottled and sealed beverages.

Since the beginning of the adventure, my parents had been steadily against it, and now I understand their reasons. Soon enough, I understood that that was not my world and that I had nothing to share with the people who ordinarily populated the club every weekend. The amount of illicit substances, once again, made me uncomfortable, and I realized I did not want to be a part of such an enterprise.

Furthermore, there was much unwanted attention from the male supervisors, and I learned that it was normal for a girl to uplift her position or have extra privileges in exchange for sexual favours. Battling for feminism and women's rights on a daily basis, needless to say, it was time for me to terminate that journey and say farewell to the field of nightlife.

The latter motivation left me upset and uneasy. I learned first-hand how these dynamics had been considered too normal in many circumstances. On this occasion, I started to think that I did not see myself living in Italy for the time being.

CHAPTER 10

OFFLINE

We are too connected to the internet and our smartphones; that is a fact. It is also true that it is extremely hard to be left behind in terms of technology. Even if we want to keep using a certain operating system or a smartphone, sooner or later, that one will become obsolete, hence not suitable for our everyday life and work and forcing us to keep being updated.

Like most working people, technology and a smartphone are crucial in my profession. I had to deal with the marketing part of my job in the first place, as promoting my business normally is the first key step in the process.

Generally, people suffering from anxiety find that technology can be overwhelming at times. For example, we need to be available 24/7 or respond to anyone as quickly as possible. Sometimes I felt overwhelmed or even powerless in the face of fast-progressing technology, precisely by the urge to be in the moment and reply to someone as fast as possible. I have learned to maintain a calm mind by not paying too much attention to the phone, checking my messages and emails every few hours during my working days, and being more physically present for the people dear to me on my days off.

It is very important to get in touch with new and existing clients and communicate with them daily. Finally, I also need technology and a good connection in order to follow up with the bookkeeping, shopping for supplies, and general office work.

I remember, however, one time when I had to start an exciting new job, but the internet had been down, and I was not able to communicate with the client and update them about my position or if I had any issues. I have learned that in these cases, or when on the other line the customer is not responding to any call or text, often there would be no bell on the door, no intuitive method of entry, and no clear sign of a code locker where usually keys are kept safe for the trade workers.

Luckily, at that time, the issue of the internet had been restored, and everything went for the better. However, that episode made me think about a surreal experience that had happened to me a few years earlier during a business trip to Italy.

On one of the first days of that trip, I locked my iPhone due to a simple and silly mistake: I had confused my personal passcode with the pin number of my Italian SIM card. This happened because of a mix of tiredness, jet lag, and stress due to a hard situation I had to deal with. After several attempts at inserting the wrong code, the phone was blocked.

I didn't have another device with me; unfortunately, I had been naive enough to think that an iPhone would have been enough for the length of my trip.

So, what does it mean to be cut off from the Internet? After the initial panic of the first day, desperation and a few cries, you really realize how we depend on our technology, and it was scary to feel that emptiness. You don't have any news or updates from the world;

according to all the social media, it feels like you are dead. If you have a pending meeting or business, it's impossible to follow up, and the other party might think less of you in case of any missed meeting or other issues.

Not having access to all my contacts, photos, emails and social media, and, most importantly, being unable to communicate with my husband, was pretty hard. After the initial shock, I could only walk to my brother-in-law's house and explain the situation. After checking on some tutorials, the best thing we could do was link my iPhone to their laptop with iTunes. Meanwhile, it was getting late, so luckily, with my niece's contacts, I managed to book an appointment with the local IT technician for the next day. The good thing about living in a small village is that everyone knows everyone, and it is easy to contact someone, especially in an emergency.

On day two of my forced digital detox, I woke up without touching, holding, or looking at my smartphone. This hadn't happened in years.

I had found an old laptop among my belongings, so I tried to use it without success.

It was really old. In the house I was staying in, I didn't have any connection to Wi-Fi, so the only thing that the laptop was useful for was looking at some old photos.

The IT appointment had been scheduled on that afternoon, and the technician told me that we could give it a try with the help of my husband's iPad from Melbourne. So, I left my iPhone to the technician for him to work his magic and headed to my niece's house. She had kindly proposed loaning me the laptop to check emails and communicate with my husband, whom I had called after seeing the technician. I still remember how upset I was during that call; I had been in a tragic mood. After all the bureaucratic madness that happened to me and led me to that trip, I wasn't sure that I could cope with this problem, too, and being cut off from the world.

Luckily my husband is my rock, and he did everything to lift me up and assured me that everything would be sorted out.

On that trip, I also remember going to my long-term doctor, the kind and caring family general practitioner who had known me for my entire life. I had been having, once again, intolerable stomach pains, and without even visiting me, he had told me that I had gastritis and severe anxiety.

That was not news to me. My upset tummy started when I was a little girl, and throughout my life, my stomach has been a filter, absorbing all the negativity, hatred and instability. The result was often excruciating pain, sometimes even resulting in me bending from the pain and the impossibility of walking.

On the third day without a smartphone, I started seeing the beauty of the world again, the simple life the older generations knew so well. Without my face pressed onto a phone, I actually lifted my head and looked at the beautiful sky, at the surrounding nature, at the colourful flowers, at the beautiful little stream of our little mountain village, and I finally breathed. On that day, I also found an old Blackberry in a drawer and started using this phone for emergencies. I had scheduled my appointments for the next day, having only offline calls and texts available on that mobile phone.

On the last day without technology, I received the news from the technician that the problem had been solved. Thanks to the technician's long and patient job of resetting, connecting it to another device, and setting new passwords, my iPhone was unlocked. I held my smartphone in my hands again right when I started to enjoy the simple life, seeing the world for what it was without a device in front of me as a filter and savouring a sort of modern freedom.

This feeling reminded me so much of my Russian summer holidays before we were trapped by technology and personal devices. Life was simpler, more genuine, and everyone seemed happier.

* * *

One thing that still strikes me often at work is the difference between housing sizes. In the Russian city I am familiar with, there were only tall buildings (also known as Stalinist architecture) containing many standard units. Those flats were mainly classified as two-bedroomed apartments, but in reality, there was one bedroom suited as a living room, one more bedroom, a tiny kitchen, a bathroom, and a little entrance hall. Entire families of four or five lived there, often even with the presence of one or both grandparents. The personal space was obviously non-existent, and there was only space available for essential things; people did not have much, but they were happier.

On the other hand, in Australia, most of the homes are spacious, maybe ten times bigger than those tiny communist flats, if not bigger. Naturally, that much room for an average family of four or five leads to extreme consumerism and owning countless things people don't even use or need. And this is a real nightmare for a housekeeper.

In my entire career, I would say that, in my opinion, two-thirds of the properties I have worked in had too much junk.

When a house is too full of stuff, it is hard for me to move and use my equipment. Every time I would risk bumping into something, and even though it never happened to me, this could have also been a matter of insurance if something broke.

Surfaces with too many items means removing or moving everything, cleaning underneath, and putting everything back in its place. This usually takes three times longer than cleaning and dusting a decluttered home. Vacuuming is not an enjoyable task either, considering again that I had to move most of the things placed on the floor, vacuum, and then move everything again. This sequence would have to be repeated once again when mopping the floors.

Many clients have had tons of boxes or bags on the ground, too, apart from the layers and layers of things on desks, drawers, benches and tables in every room. Every corner, every chair, and every door handle could be full of shopping bags, random boxes, or backpacks.

Countless times I tried to jealously organize and clear up a particular corner, for example, in the laundry room, to have some room to work within, only to find that space piled with layers of clutter on my next visit.

Personally, I try my best to have a minimalist and clean approach to my home life, buying and owning what my family really needs and getting rid of items we don't need anymore, or donating to charities once or twice a year. Many gurus have defined minimalism as a lifestyle practice focused on decreasing distractions that keep you from doing what matters to you. It is also proven that good energy needs space in order to flow, so having every room inside our homes full of junk will not bring positivity and a clear mind.

Furthermore, minimalism is all about owning only what adds value and meaning to our life, as well as the lives of the people we care about, and getting rid of the rest. It's about removing the clutter and using our time and energy for the things that matter. We only have a certain amount of energy, time, and space in our lives. In order to make the most of it, we must be conscious about the way we live.

I am also very considerate about our planet and try to live as sustainably as possible, choosing to significantly decrease my household's weekly waste, recycle whenever I can, and be meticulous about the rubbish and recycling programs.

However, those who own an exaggerated amount of things and a big house, as a consequence, usually also have a large quantity of rubbish.

In Melbourne, each council normally allocates one outdoor bin of general waste, one recycling bin, and one green organic waste per household. In many cases, these are not enough for an average household.

I remember when I was little, in Russia, we had a very little amount of rubbish in my grandparents' apartment. There were few public waste bins in the courtyard that covered the nearest apartment blocks. Four or five rudimentary steel containers were available for hundreds if not thousands of residents, and I never saw those bins completely full.

Sometimes someone would leave some old and broken household items on the side, and a few times, I witnessed some disadvantaged neighbour rummaging through those items, looking for a little treasure to keep.

In my eyes, these simple, often very poor families were genuinely happy deep down, despite owning very little and leading a simple lifestyle. Whilst we, in our modern western society dominated by capitalism, are surrounded by everything we don't even need, are always looking to purchase something else, and it seems like our happiness is dictated by objects rather than emotions.

It is a strong statement I sometimes use but looking at the society in modern and advantaged countries, I feel that we will be buried under our own rubbish sooner or later.

In my Italian hometown, the situation is similar. I understand that I can only share the experience of the little town I lived in, but I am proud to have resided in an area in northern Italy famous for its green and environmentally friendly initiatives. Apart from the advanced research and campaigns, the residents made a great difference by, once again, following the rules and differentiating their waste, limiting their consumption and spending, and generally buying what was really necessary for a household. The houses there are also pretty tiny, and usually, people live in standard-sized apartments. Lastly, in northern Italy, wintertime can be very cold and harsh, so it is easier and more economical to heat up a smaller residence rather than a large one.

* * *

Workwise, this sensation of being cut off from a vital service reminded me of another experience I had. I was regularly working for a young family living in a tall building in the inner-city suburbs. It was a two-bedroom and two-bathroom average-size apartment, and the job had always been straightforward. One day, however, I noticed that there was no electricity in the whole building, counting about 400 apartments.

Hence, I was not able to work on that occasion and skipped the session; however, my clients kept me in the loop about the building updates. Apparently, due to a water leakage, there was no power in the building for days. Most residents and guests staying in the short-term serviced apartments had been placed in temporary hotels or accommodations, all of that costing the management millions of dollars, on top of the greatest inconvenience.

A whole crew of electricians and other technicians had to work tirelessly for a few days, 24 hours per day, in order to fix the problem. In the end, the problem had been indeed a water leakage, due to someone flushing a whole can of soft drink in the toilet. Without all the judgment and with all the open-mindedness and understanding that many cultures might be different from mine, I still ask how anyone could think of doing something so dumb as flushing a can in a toilet, causing distress to potentially thousands of people and costing the management and insurances millions of dollars.

* * *

Being disconnected from the web also reminded me of a proposal to clean a client's friend's boat. I have never had a similar experience, and despite my curiosity and willingness to add a diverse new project to my portfolio, I declined due to my tight schedule and inconvenient location. The vessel's subject, however, brought back a memory of my childhood.

In the area of my grandparents' Dacha, there was a place everyone in local slang called "the sea." It was not a sea, as a matter of fact, but a little lake or stream overlooking some other Dachas, and it was located around half an hour's walk from our own summer residence.

The first sight of that place was far from a luxurious lake resort; on the contrary, it reminded me of an illegal dump area. On the shore, there were many large truck tyres, steel poles, and other hard waste materials. It was an exercise of survival, not getting hurt among these rigid materials.

The bottom of this little lake was repugnantly soft, but despite the potentially toxic and questionably secure area, all the kids living nearby were happy to swim and play all together in the water. The massive rubber tyres were like carousels on which have so much fun.

On the same shore, there was also an abandoned ship. My granddad would gladly take me on the vessel's tour, which must have been war wreckage. We would look over the hull, passing through the captain's desk and all the little cabins, finishing the tour by admiring the keel. During the tour, my special tour guide would make up a brave history tale about how that boat had been crucial to a particular national achievement in past years.

My grandfather was a very wise, tough and courageous man and was extremely curious about knowledge. He would often proudly teach me lessons about history or geography. He had a very harsh upbringing. He never knew his parents and resided throughout his childhood in foster care. Once he reached working age, he moved out of the guardianship and sought employment at the local factories, which was customary in the Soviet era.

My Russian grandparents were the only ones I had, and I always carry their sweet memories, lessons, and legacy with me.

They passed away a few years ago peacefully, within a few days of each other.

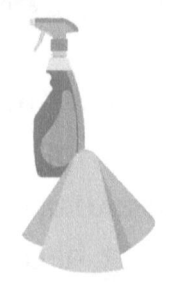

CHAPTER 11

PANDEMIC

Balance is everything in leading a happy and healthy life. I have never had any balance in my life; on the contrary, I have been a mess emotionally, physically and mentally.

A few years ago, however, the time to change my life arrived, and there was no looking back.

I started my counselling journey with a therapist, and it has been the best gift I could ever have given to myself. An experience like this is worth it even just to understand ourselves better, our mindset, and our behaviour, let alone if there is a huge shadow impinging on our reality. We can try and carry on with our lives, but this shadow is always present, and whether we do something good or something bad, it is always here, following us in the darkest moments.

It was a relief to break my family's cycle and finally give a name to what had been haunting me for all my life. I had started to understand how I saw reality through a filter of negativity and to realize how my mindset needed to change.

This new well-being and balance, however, was interrupted by something we all still remember very well: the start of the COVID-19 pandemic. Across the world, every single one of us was impacted straight away by this scary new reality.

Australia is a relatively distant country, so at the beginning, most of its residents didn't think this new virus would reach us, and we also did not know how powerful it would be: everyone thought it would pass within a couple of months.

Soon enough, however, within a few weeks of the global outbreak and a few confirmed cases, the Australian government took the decision to close its international borders to everyone but citizens and permanent residents. Those finding themselves overseas were encouraged to come back home as soon as possible, whilst all the individuals residing in Australia on visas were encouraged to leave the country for the time being. The number of international flights available was reduced drastically in a matter of days, and a mandatory hotel quarantine of two weeks was introduced for everyone entering the country.

Nevertheless, for all Australia's citizens and permanent residents, leaving the country was not allowed. We would need to request special permission, which was very hard to get. But most importantly, it would be close to impossible to book a flight and come back. There were caps for every arriving flight; some of the biggest airplanes carried only twenty or so passengers. Furthermore, everyone entering the country had to undergo a mandatory hotel quarantine for two weeks, sometimes stuck in a room without fresh air.

Workwise, the professional who was not able to work from home had to hold a travel permit. Luckily, cleaning businesses were among the essential services, and those employed in these services, like me, could offer assistance with a work exemption document.

Whilst domestic cleaning was not permitted, commercial cleaning for certain enterprises was allowed with this paperwork. Throughout the lockdowns, the authorities have never stopped and checked me.

As a migrant myself, it was unbearable. My husband and I often travelled to Europe, as most new migrants living in Australia did.

To many, like me, this has been one of the hardest parts, the unknown, the loss of a well-established balance, and all the restrictions that would come.

In the following year and a half, Melbourne would have six lockdowns, for a total of more than 260 days, among the countries hitting a world record.

During worldwide summers and Australian winters, I remember that the world was pretty much business as usual; everyone travelled freely, went on holidays, and had a life with little to no restrictions. It is also true that the restriction would come back in most countries with the arrival of the cold season, but at least everyone could have a little break from the madness of this virus during the summertime.

Australians did not have that luck. We were closed internationally for nearly two years and tried to live through the uncertainty that all those six lockdowns brought us.

I noticed that the pandemic and the numerous lockdowns brought out the best or the worst of who we are as human beings.

While many had started to take comfort in joining freedom protests, following the so-called health experts or virologists on YouTube, and agreeing with conspiracy theories, the vaccine was the only concrete way out of the nightmare of the virus. The vaccination program in Australia started relatively later than the rest of the world; however, it was very effective and progressed quickly.

At one stage, the number of vaccines administered grew substantially daily, so every milestone brought to the population more and more easing of restrictions.

The last restriction to fall was the opening of the Australian borders, hence the restart of international flights.

My husband and I booked our post-pandemic flight to Italy on the exact day of the announcement of the reopening of the international borders.

After two hard years and two months, we were ready to board an international flight to our hometown, and that feeling was among the best feelings of our lives. The idea of flying back to Europe once again was so powerful that we decided to surprise our dearest one!

After a pandemic, after the longest lockdown on the planet, with six lockdowns in the city of Melbourne, there was light at the end of the tunnel after one of the darkest periods of my life.

In recent years, I learned the importance of mental well-being and how our body tells us what our mind is not ready to accept. Unfortunately, many individuals are still skeptical about psychotherapy, and mine is a perfect example for them.

* * *

The word "mother" had always had a negative connotation for me. Only when I found out that I was expecting my first son myself could I finally pronounce this word with joy and positivity.

Many new mums who had broken families, especially absent mother figures, had many doubts and fears about motherhood. Furthermore, if a mental health condition is present in the family history, new mothers are genetically more likely to suffer from postpartum depression and anxiety.

That, however, did not happen to me, strangely. I knew that my feelings for my child would be so full of unconditional love that this would overshadow every negative feeling. For the lack of guidance and parental figure I never had, I would take that as an example of what to avoid in order to give my very best. I vowed to be the mother I never had to my son.

I had the blessing of an easy and healthy pregnancy, where I felt every day on cloud nine. In a weird way, it felt like I was experiencing the pain and sickness typical of pregnancy throughout my life, but not during the actual time of carrying my baby inside me.

* * *

When I was twenty years old, I had a horrible car accident, one of those situations where you are alive, thanks to a miracle. I still struggle to speak about it now, and it is hard to go into all the details.

In the evening on the day of the accident, I planned to catch up with some friends met during the summer in the city of Verona, about one and a half hours from where I was living then. We all had a lovely time in the charming city centre of the city of Romeo and Juliet, and soon after, it was time for me to drive back home. I was the driver and was alone in my car. A few kilometers from home, my car went off the road and, after a massive flight, landed in the little stream on the side of the main road.

I saw moments of my life passing through my mind, and I thought I had already rekindled with my beloved friends, understanding with terror what my friend Virginia had been through during her own car crash.

I remember driving on that same road around a week prior to the accident, noticing that the stream had been full of rainwater. If the accident had happened only a few days earlier, I would have surely drowned, trapped in the wreckage of the car. Only one week later, though, miraculously, there was just a little bit of rainwater.

I remember the darkness; I remember the shock; I remember the numbness. What I do not remember is how I got to the hospital. The first thing I saw there was a doctor trying to ask me questions, and the second was my parents in the corridor. My father was pale from worry, and my mother was shouting, pointing at me, and surely stating what a disappointment I was and that I could have done better by not surviving the accident at all.

Still numb from the pain, before completely realizing what had happened, once again, I only felt rejected, hated and alone.

In that moment, I vowed that no matter how dark things turned, I would always find my light.

My husband has been my rock throughout our life together. He accepted and loved me unconditionally and supported me in every journey and through the ups and downs of life.

During our post-pandemic winter holiday in Italy, my husband and I spent a couple of days in Verona. I have only positive memories of this town in the heart of Veneto's region; after all, it is famous for its decadent food and wine, its rich history and landmarks, as a shopping destination, and, of course, the city of Shakespeare's Romeo and Juliet.

I have chosen to focus on love, which always wins.

In Verona, I found out I was expecting my first child. So many years after that accident, I finally found my light after some very dark moments.

In fact, I have found life in the place I thought I would die.

A big lesson the pandemic has taught us is gratefulness for little or big things. First, we need to appreciate our health, which is our biggest wealth. We should not take for granted our loved ones, and we should always try to communicate our feelings. A few kind words go a long way.

Once again, I understood that physical things don't matter much; they are only items we don't need and take our attention away from more important issues.

With my mind and body grateful for whom I have become today, I have often thought about a way to repay my latest hometown, Australia, for everything it has given me.

This country has accepted me unconditionally, given me a place to call home after feeling so lost, and taught me once again that nothing comes for free, but hard work always pays off.

Australia confirmed to me how many beautiful cultures there are in the world and that we all need to open our minds in order to see that our home countries, customs, or mindsets are not the only ones in this world and may not be the right ones for us.

And suddenly, just like that, I realized how I could give back to Australia: by creating a new life and raising my son as an Australian.

I have already put my trust in constructing a career in this country, a place of peace, respect and opportunities. Now it was time to expand what my family has achieved through the years to our child.

As a parent, it is comforting to know that my son will always be accepted, supported and welcomed. I am lucky to live in a family-friendly country with many programs and initiatives for children and parents.

My wish for the future is to continue to be happy, loved and at peace.

After all the darkness, I have found my light after all.

www.ingramcontent.com/pod-product-compliance
Lightning Source LLC
LaVergne TN
LVHW041637060526
838200LV00040B/1604